Contents

Japanese Crab & Radish Salad (recipe on page 24)

Special Features

Ingredients for Carefree Cooking

Saving time and trouble in the kitchen has become a top priority for many cooks today. But while everyone strives for convenience, no one wants to give up great taste. Is there really such a thing as a fast, easy-to-make recipe that tastes delicious, too?

Indeed there is. In fact, you'll find over 130 such recipes to tempt you in the pages ahead. For every recipe, we've kept the number of ingredients to six or fewer, which shortcuts the often time-consuming process of shopping, assembly, and preparation. As an added bonus, nearly all our recipes go from start to finish in no more than 30 minutes. To make life even easier, we give menu suggestions, preparation and cooking times, and a nutritional analysis for every recipe.

It all adds up to a simple, healthy, and exciting way to cook. For weeknight meals or casual entertaining, company dinners or lazy weekend brunches, the six-ingredient formula will work wonders for you.

Keep It Short

A quick glance at any recipe in this book reveals a short list of ingredients. This trims more than just the length of the recipe.

For one thing, it's likely that you'll have on hand most of the ingredients you'll need for a recipe. Even if you don't, meal-planning and shopping time can be significantly reduced—there are fewer items to jot down, purchase, and put away, even if you shop for several meals at one time.

A short ingredient list also cuts down assembly time. Once you've read through the recipe (the first step in efficient cooking), you can quickly gather together what you'll need. (No recipe requires advance chilling or precooking, so there's no make-ahead work.)

Because fewer ingredients go into the bowl or pan, preparation is speeded up. You won't need to spend a lot of time rinsing, chopping, mixing, and measuring. And once you're ready to cook, it will take a maximum of 30 minutes (some dishes require no cooking at all). Even after a busy day, you can have a fresh, homemade meal on the table and still have plenty of energy—and time— left to enjoy it!

Keep It Simple

The more sophisticated we become, the more we seem to appreciate simplicity. This is obvious in the art of cooking, where uncomplicated recipes, simple ingredients, and easy cooking techniques are often the keys to superb dishes.

By design, the recipes in this book are simple to use. You can scan the ingredient list instantly; it appears on one side of the recipe, with the ingredients clearly marked with colored boxes (■). Water, salt, pepper, and optional ingredients are not counted. The step-by-step instructions are numbered so they're easy to follow.

These recipes are based on fresh, easy-to-find, and naturally delicious ingredients.

They're put together creatively, relying on familiar techniques and producing tantalizing results. Presentation is simple because garnishes are always optional; they add a flourish if desired, but the food still tastes delicious and looks attractive without them.

Keep It Delicious

In dozens of ways, this book proves that culinary success is not measured by the clock or by recipe length.

No matter how simple or complex, all good cooking starts with ingredients of top quality. This book shows you how to put them together to create irresistible pasta and egg dishes, appetizing soups and salads, grilled specialties, bountiful breakfasts, and a host of other choices to tempt family and friends— and with very little trouble.

Taste for yourself. Once you've discovered the joy of cooking with six ingredients or less, you'll look forward to it no matter what the occasion.

A Word About Our Nutritional Data

For our recipes, we provide a nutritional analysis stating calorie count; grams of protein, carbohydrates, and total fat; and milligrams of cholesterol and sodium. Generally, the nutritional information applies to a single serving, based on the largest number of servings given for each recipe.

The nutritional analysis does not include optional ingredients or those for which no specific amount is stated. If an ingredient is listed with an option, the information was calculated using the first choice. Likewise, if a range is given for the amount of an ingredient, values were figured based on the first, lower amount.

Two kinds of onion give bold emphasis to the wine-vinegar dip in Shrimp with Tart Dipping Sauce (recipe on facing page). A chive tie decorates each shrimp.

Appetizers

To prepare a quick nibble when guests drop in or while dinner cooks, look to the no-fuss recipes in this chapter. No longer does convenience necessarily mean relying on a can of nuts or an uninspiring brick of cheese. In the next pages, you'll find an exciting repertoire of appetizers, some simple and some sophisticated enough for a company buffet—but none that require more than a handful of ingredients or any complex preparation techniques.

Shrimp with Tart Dipping Sauce

Pictured on facing page

Preparation time: About 25 minutes
Cooking time: 3 to 4 minutes

Plump pink shrimp, tied with vivid chive sashes, taste as delicious as they look when dipped into a sauce. Serve as an hors d'oeuvre or first course with crisp sauvignon blanc.

- 1 **pound (about 25) medium-size shrimp, shelled and deveined**
- 35 **whole chives (*each* about 7 inches long)**
- ¼ **cup *each* dry white wine and white wine vinegar**
- 1 **tablespoon *each* minced shallots and minced chives**
- ½ **teaspoon pepper**

1 In a 2-quart pan, bring about 4 cups water to a boil over high heat. Add shrimp; reduce heat, cover, and simmer until shrimp are opaque when cut (3 to 4 minutes). Drain and immerse in cold water to stop cooking; drain again. Set aside.

2 In a medium-size frying pan, bring about 1 inch water to a boil over high heat. Add whole chives and cook just until wilted (about 5 seconds); remove immediately with tongs. Tie a chive around center of each shrimp; set aside.

3 In a small bowl, stir together wine, vinegar, shallots, minced chives, and pepper. Arrange shrimp on a serving platter and offer sauce alongside. Makes about 25 appetizers (about 8 servings).

Per appetizer: 18 calories, 3 g protein, 0.4 g carbohydrates, 0.3 g total fat, 22 mg cholesterol, 22 mg sodium

7

Garlic Mussels on the Half Shell

Preparation time: About 25 minutes
Cooking time: About 10 minutes

For taste, thrift, and easy elegance, mussels make unbeatable appetizers. Here they're presented on the half shell, topped with garlic and cheese.

- 1½ **pounds mussels, scrubbed**
- 1 **cup dry white wine**
- ¼ **cup olive oil or salad oil**
- ⅓ **cup freshly grated Parmesan cheese**
- 3 **large cloves garlic, minced or pressed**
- 1 **tablespoon finely chopped parsley**

1 Discard any mussels that don't close when tapped. Pull beard (clump of fibers along side of shell) off each mussel with a quick tug.

2 In a 5- to 6-quart pan, combine mussels and wine. Cover and simmer over medium-high heat just until shells open (about 5 minutes). Lift out with a slotted spoon, discarding any mussels that don't open. Meanwhile, stir together oil, 3 tablespoons of the cheese, and garlic; set aside.

3 When mussels are cool enough to handle, remove meat from shells, discarding half of each shell. Arrange remaining half shells in a single layer in a heatproof serving dish. Put a mussel in each shell; drizzle with oil mixture.

4 Broil mussels 4 inches below heat just until cheese begins to melt and mussels are hot (about 5 minutes). Sprinkle with parsley and remaining cheese. Serve with wooden picks. Makes about 3 dozen appetizers (about 12 servings).

Per appetizer: 25 calories, 1 g protein, 0.4 g carbohydrates, 2 g total fat, 3 mg cholesterol, 40 mg sodium

Smoked Trout with Horseradish Cream

Preparation time: About 20 minutes

Peppery watercress and a pungent horseradish dip counterbalance subtle smoked trout in this easy appetizer.

- 1 **boneless butterflied smoked trout (8 to 12 oz.)**
- **About ¼ cup large capers, drained and rinsed**
- ¾ **cup whipping cream**
- 1 **tablespoon lemon juice**
  Salt and ground white pepper
- 2 **tablespoons prepared horseradish**
  Watercress sprigs, washed and dried

1 Remove and discard skin from trout. Cut fillets in half lengthwise; then cut crosswise into ½-inch-wide strips. Place a caper in center of each strip and spear with a wooden pick; set aside.

2 Whip cream with lemon juice. Season to taste with salt and white pepper. Fold in horseradish. Transfer to a small bowl and place in center of a serving platter; surround with watercress. Arrange trout on watercress. Makes about 4 dozen appetizers (12 to 16 servings).

Per appetizer: 17 calories, 1 g protein, 0.2 g carbohydrates, 1 g total fat, 8 mg cholesterol, 56 mg sodium

Basil Meatballs

Pictured on Page 11

Preparation time: About 10 minutes
Grilling time: 10 to 15 minutes

It's both fun and easy to serve appetizers—such as these skewers of subtly seasoned, basil-wrapped meatballs—hot off the grill. Also provide Beaujolais wine and sliced, buttered baguettes.

- **1 pound bulk pork sausage**
- **½ cup minced fresh basil leaves**
- **1 teaspoon crushed fennel seeds**
- **20 to 25 large fresh basil leaves**

1 Mix together sausage, minced basil, and fennel seeds. Shape into 1-inch balls.

2 Wrap a basil leaf around each meatball, lightly pressing it into meat so it sticks (leaf does not have to cover entire meatball). Thread 2 or 3 meatballs closely together on long, slender skewers.

3 Lay skewers on a grill 2 to 4 inches above a solid bed of hot coals (extinguish any flares with a spray of water). Grill, turning every 2 to 3 minutes, until meatballs are no longer pink in center when cut (10 to 15 minutes). Serve on skewers. Makes 8 servings.

Per serving: 109 calories, 6 g protein, 2 g carbohydrates, 9 g total fat, 22 mg cholesterol, 349 mg sodium

Prosciutto & Pea Bundles

Preparation time: 20 minutes
Cooking time: About 30 seconds

Naturally shaped for filling, crunchy sugar snap peas become attractive hors d'oeuvres when bundled with carrot and prosciutto.

- **60 sugar snap peas, ends and strings removed**
- **2 medium-size carrots, peeled**
- **2 to 3 ounces thinly sliced prosciutto or cooked ham**
- **1 package (4 oz.) onion-flavored spreadable cream cheese**

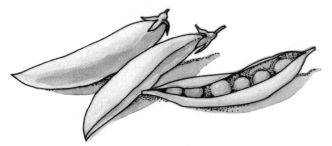

1 In a wide frying pan, bring 2 inches water to a boil over high heat. Add peas and cook, uncovered, until bright green (about 30 seconds). Drain and plunge into ice water, stirring until peas are cool. Drain again and set aside.

2 Cut carrots crosswise into thirds; cut each third into 10 matchstick-size pieces. Cut prosciutto into 60 strips.

3 With a sharp knife, slice each pea along outside seam. Open slightly and push about ½ teaspoon of the cheese into each, smoothing cheese with back of a knife. Position a carrot stick on filling, hold in place, and wrap prosciutto in a band around carrot and pea to secure. Repeat until all peas are wrapped. Makes 60 bundles (10 to 12 servings).

Per bundle: 10 calories, 0.5 g protein, 0.6 g carbohydrates, 0.7 g total fat, 2 mg cholesterol, 24 mg sodium

Eggplant & Goat Cheese Rolls

Pictured on facing page

Preparation time: About 15 minutes
Baking time: About 13 minutes

Begin a wide-awake brunch with these goat cheese, watercress, and eggplant rolls accompanied with breadsticks and spicy Bloody Marys. If available, select long, slender Oriental eggplants, which are generally sweeter and have smaller seeds than the regular kind.

- ■ **1 pound Oriental eggplants (about 4 *total*) or regular eggplant, stems removed**
- ■ **1½ tablespoons olive oil**
- ■ **3 ounces soft goat cheese, such as Montrachet**
- ■ **12 to 16 watercress sprigs, washed and dried**

 Cut eggplants lengthwise into ¼- to ⅓-inch-thick slices (if using regular variety, cut slices in half lengthwise). Brush both sides with oil and place in a single layer on large baking sheets. Bake in a 450° oven for 8 minutes; turn and continue baking until very soft when pressed (about 5 more minutes). Remove from pans and let cool.

2 Place about ½ teaspoon of the cheese at one end of each eggplant slice; top with a sprig of watercress, letting leaves overhang edges. Roll up. Arrange on a serving platter. Makes 12 to 16 rolls (4 to 6 servings).

Per roll: 101 calories, 4 g protein, 6 g carbohydrates, 7 g total fat, 75 mg cholesterol, 92 mg sodium

---

Sweet Onions on Herb Toast

Preparation time: About 15 minutes
Cooking time: About 20 minutes

Mellow, slow-cooked onions contrast deliciously with tangy goat cheese and prosciutto in this sophisticated appetizer. Accompany with chilled white wine or champagne.

- ■ **4 tablespoons butter or margarine**
- ■ **3 large onions, thinly sliced**
- ■ **1 teaspoon fresh thyme leaves or ½ teaspoon dry thyme leaves**
- ■ **24 cocktail-size rye bread slices**
- ■ **2 ounces thinly sliced prosciutto, slivered**
- ■ **¼ pound mild goat cheese, such as Montrachet or bûcheron, crumbled**

1 In a wide frying pan, melt 2 tablespoons of the butter over medium heat. Add onions and cook, stirring often, until golden and very limp (about 20 minutes).

2 Meanwhile, melt remaining 2 tablespoons butter in a small pan; stir in thyme and set aside. Place bread slices in a single layer on 2 large baking sheets. Broil 4 inches below heat until lightly browned; turn, brush with butter mixture, and continue broiling until golden (2 to 4 minutes total). Set aside.

3 Add prosciutto and cheese to onions and stir until cheese is melted. Spread evenly on bread. Arrange on a serving platter. Makes 24 appetizers (6 to 8 servings).

Per appetizer: 62 calories, 2 g protein, 5 g carbohydrates, 4 g total fat 11 mg cholesterol, 140 mg sodium

Hot and cool hors d'oeuvres served with lemonade
are (clockwise from left) Snow Peas with Mint
Sauce (recipe on page 12), Basil Meatballs
(recipe on page 9), and Eggplant & Goat Cheese
Rolls (recipe on facing page).

Baby Artichokes
with Blue Cheese

Preparation time: About 15 minutes
Cooking time: 20 to 25 minutes

You won't be able to resist these pop-in-the-mouth hors d'oeuvres. Removing their coarse leaves makes the cooked artichokes completely edible; the blue cheese topping adds tantalizing flavor.

- ■ 2 tablespoons vinegar or lemon juice
- ■ 12 small artichokes (2 inches in diameter)
- ■ ¼ cup butter or margarine, at room temperature
- ■ 3 ounces blue-veined cheese, crumbled

1 In a 4- to 5-quart pan, mix vinegar with about 2 quarts water. Break off and discard artichoke leaves down to tender pale yellow leaves. Cut off thorny tips; trim stems flush with bottoms and lightly peel bottoms. Drop artichokes into pan.

2 Bring water mixture to a boil over high heat; reduce heat, cover, and simmer until artichoke bottoms are tender when pierced (10 to 15 minutes). Drain and plunge into ice water; drain again. Cut artichokes in half lengthwise.

3 Arrange, cut sides up, in a large baking pan. Mash butter and blue cheese together with a fork; spread evenly over artichokes. Bake in a 350° oven just until cheese is melted (about 10 minutes). Arrange on a serving platter. Makes 24 appetizers (4 to 6 servings).

Per appetizer: 54 calories, 2 g protein, 6 g carbohydrates, 3 g total fat, 8 mg cholesterol, 107 mg sodium

Snow Peas with
Mint Sauce
Pictured on page 11

Preparation time: About 15 minutes
Cooking time: About 30 seconds

For a fresh summertime dip idea, present crisp snow peas with cool mint sauce. With icy lemonade alongside, it's a perfect choice for patio entertaining.

- ■ 1 pound Chinese pea pods (snow or sugar peas), ends and strings removed
- ■ ¼ cup *each* sour cream and mayonnaise
- ■ 2 tablespoons coarsely chopped fresh mint leaves
        Fresh mint sprigs (optional)

1 In a wide frying pan, bring 2 inches water to a boil over high heat. Add peas and cook, uncovered, until bright green (about 30 seconds). Drain and plunge into ice water, stirring until peas are cool. Drain again. Set aside.

2 In a food processor or blender, whirl sour cream, mayonnaise, and the 2 tablespoons mint leaves until mint is finely chopped. Transfer to a small bowl, place in center of a serving platter, and surround with peas. Garnish with mint sprigs, if desired. Makes 6 servings.

Per serving: 117 calories, 2 g protein, 6 g carbohydrates, 9 g total fat, 10 mg cholesterol, 60 mg sodium

Chili Peanuts

Preparation time: About 5 minutes
Baking time: About 25 minutes

Lively Mexican flavors make these peanuts irresistible. To sip alongside, offer ice cold beer, Margarita cocktails, or tomato juice.

- 2 cups (about 11 oz.) raw Spanish peanuts
- 2 teaspoons chili powder
- 1 teaspoon ground cumin
- 3 small dried hot red chiles
- 1 tablespoon salad oil
  Salt

1 Place peanuts in a large rimmed baking pan. Bake in a 350° oven, stirring occasionally, until pale gold (about 15 minutes). Remove from oven and add chili powder, cumin, chiles, and oil; mix well.

2 Return to oven and continue baking, stirring once, until nuts are golden brown (8 to 10 more minutes). Season to taste with salt. Transfer to a serving bowl; serve warm or cool. Makes 8 to 10 servings.

Per serving: 192 calories, 8 g protein, 6 g carbohydrates, 17 g total fat, 0 mg cholesterol, 11 mg sodium

Hummus with Pita Crisps

Preparation time: About 10 minutes
Cooking time: 5 to 10 minutes

Popular in the Middle East, where many versions are prepared, this wholesome and satisfying garbanzo dip fits any informal occasion. Wash it down with minted ice tea or cold beer.

- 6 pocket breads (6 inches in diameter)
- ½ cup olive oil
  Salt and pepper
- ¼ cup sesame seeds
- 1 can (15 oz.) garbanzos, drained (reserve liquid)
- 3 tablespoons lemon juice
- 1 or 2 cloves garlic

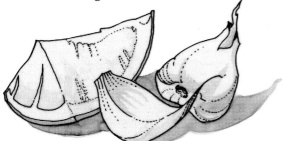

1 Split pocket breads and brush split sides with ¼ cup of the olive oil; season to taste with salt and pepper. Stack and cut into 6 to 8 wedges. Place wedges in a single layer on 2 large baking sheets. Bake in a 400° oven until crisp and golden (5 to 10 minutes). Set aside.

2 Meanwhile, in a small frying pan, toast sesame seeds over medium-low heat, shaking pan often, until golden (5 to 7 minutes). Transfer seeds to a blender or food processor and add garbanzos, 2 more tablespoons of the oil, lemon juice, garlic, and 6 tablespoons of the reserved garbanzo liquid. Whirl, adding more liquid if needed, until hummus is smooth but still thick enough to hold its shape. Season to taste with salt and pepper.

3 Transfer hummus to a serving bowl and drizzle with remaining 2 tablespoons oil. Serve with pita wedges to scoop up. Makes 6 to 8 servings.

Per serving: 341 calories, 8 g protein, 41 g carbohydrates, 17 g total fat, 0 mg cholesterol, 433 mg sodium

Easy to make and smooth to sip, Creamy
Potato Watercress Bisque (recipe on facing page) owes
its velvety texture to sour cream, its assertiveness to
green onions. A sprinkling of ham adds substance.

14

Soups

Especially in wintertime, the thought of piping hot soup awakens appetites. But there's more to soup than just comfort on a chilly night. Served with crusty bread and salad, soup is often the easiest choice for a satisfying meal.

In this chapter you'll find cold soups to serve in summer, invigorating soups made with spring's bounty, and hale and hearty soups that please in all seasons. Whether offered as the meal starter or the main course, wonderful soups bring even the simplest menu to life.

Creamy Potato Watercress Bisque

Pictured on facing page

Preparation time: About 15 minutes
Cooking time: 20 to 25 minutes

Substantial enough to serve as a meal-in-a-bowl with bread and cheese, this puréed soup also makes a festive starter for holiday dinners. A finishing touch of chopped ham adds contrasting color and flavor.

- **3 cups regular-strength chicken broth**
- **2 large thin-skinned potatoes (about 1 lb. *total*), peeled and cut into 1-inch chunks**
- **2 cups lightly packed watercress sprigs, rinsed and drained**
- **1 cup sour cream**
- **3 green onions (including tops), thinly sliced**
  Salt and ground white pepper
- **¼ pound thinly sliced cooked ham, chopped**

1 In a 3- to 4-quart pan, bring broth and potatoes to a boil over high heat; reduce heat, cover, and simmer until potatoes are tender when pierced (15 to 20 minutes).

2 Reserve 4 of the watercress sprigs for garnish. In a blender or food processor, whirl remaining watercress, sour cream, green onions, and broth mixture, a portion at a time, until puréed. Season to taste with salt and white pepper.

3 Return soup to pan and stir over medium heat just until hot. Ladle soup into wide, shallow bowls. Top each serving with a mound of ham and a watercress sprig. Makes 4 servings.

Per serving: 284 calories, 13 g protein, 23 g carbohydrates, 16 g total fat, 42 mg cholesterol, 1,224 mg sodium

Mushroom-Tarragon Bisque

Preparation time: About 10 minutes
Cooking time: About 15 minutes

Earthy in character, this comforting soup goes well with Chicken & Cheese Subs (page 61) or other hearty sandwiches for Sunday supper.

- **1 pound mushrooms, cleaned and ends trimmed**
- **4 cups regular-strength chicken broth**
- **¼ cup lightly packed fresh tarragon**
- **½ cup whipping cream**

1 Set aside 2 of the mushrooms for garnish. In a blender or food processor, whirl remaining mushrooms, broth, and 2 tablespoons of the tarragon, half at a time, until mushrooms are finely chopped.

2 In a 3- to 4-quart pan, bring broth mixture to a boil over high heat. Reduce heat, cover, and simmer until mushrooms are soft (about 10 minutes).

3 Add cream and stir just until hot. Ladle soup into bowls. Slice reserved mushrooms. Sprinkle mushrooms and remaining tarragon over each portion. Makes 4 servings.

Per serving: 151 calories, 5 g protein, 9 g carbohydrates, 12 g total fat, 33 mg cholesterol, 1,019 mg sodium

Sausage & Kale Soup

Preparation time: About 15 minutes
Cooking time: 20 to 25 minutes

Round out this robust soup with pumpernickel bread and sweet butter. Alongside, offer hearty ale or apple cider, and your simple supper is complete.

- **1 pound linguisa sausage, cut diagonally into ¼-inch-thick slices**
- **1 large onion, chopped**
- **2 large carrots, peeled and chopped**
- **10 cups regular-strength chicken broth**
- **¾ pound kale, tough stems trimmed**
  Salt and pepper

1 In a 5- to 6-quart pan, cook sausage, stirring, over high heat until browned (8 to 10 minutes). Discard all but 2 tablespoons of the drippings.

2 Add onion and carrots to drippings in pan and cook, stirring, until onion is soft (about 5 minutes). Add broth. Cover and bring to a boil.

3 Meanwhile, rinse and drain kale. Cut crosswise into ½-inch-wide strips. Add to boiling broth and cook, stirring, until limp and bright green (3 to 5 minutes). Season to taste with salt and pepper. Transfer to a large tureen or ladle into bowls. Makes 6 to 8 servings.

Per serving: 210 calories, 12 g protein, 11 g carbohydrates, 14 g total fat, 34 mg cholesterol, 1,464 mg sodium

Maritata

Preparation time: About 10 minutes
Cooking time: About 10 minutes

Maritata, which means married in Italian, joins broth, cheese, egg yolks, and cream in an elegant first-course offering. Follow it with roast chicken and sautéed peppers for an impressive dinner.

- 6 cups regular-strength chicken broth
- ⅓ cup dry tiny pasta (pastina); or 2 ounces dry vermicelli, broken into short lengths
- ½ cup (¼ lb.) unsalted butter, at room temperature
- 1 cup (about 5 oz.) freshly grated Parmesan cheese
- 4 egg yolks
- 1 cup whipping cream
  Ground nutmeg (optional)

1 In a 4- to 5-quart pan, bring broth to a boil over high heat. Add pasta, reduce heat to medium, and simmer, uncovered, just until pasta is al dente (about 3 minutes).

2 Meanwhile, in a bowl or food processor, blend butter, cheese, and egg yolks until smooth; blend in cream.

3 Slowly pour about 1 cup of the simmering broth into egg mixture, beating constantly. Then return egg-broth mixture to pan, beating constantly until hot (2 to 3 minutes). Ladle soup into bowls. Dust each serving with nutmeg, if desired. Makes 4 to 6 servings.

Per serving: 454 calories, 15 g protein, 11 g carbohydrates, 40 g total fat, 283 mg cholesterol, 1,404 mg sodium

Corn Chowder

Preparation time: About 10 minutes
Cooking time: About 30 minutes

This all-American summer chowder goes well with another national favorite—grilled hamburgers, complete with fixings. Because this recipe calls for canned cream-style corn, you can enjoy this version the year around.

- 8 slices bacon
- 1 large onion, chopped
- 4 cups *each* water and peeled, diced thin-skinned potatoes
- 2 cans (about 1 lb. *each*) cream-style corn
- 4 cups milk or 2 cups *each* milk and half-and-half
  Salt and pepper
- 2 tablespoons butter or margarine (optional)

1 In a 5- to 6-quart pan, cook bacon over medium-high heat until crisp (about 7 minutes). Drain on paper towels, crumble, and set aside; discard all but 2 tablespoons of the drippings.

2 Add onion to drippings in pan and cook, stirring, until soft (5 minutes). Add water, potatoes, and corn. Bring to a boil over high heat; reduce heat, cover, and simmer until potatoes are tender when pierced (about 15 minutes).

3 Stir in milk and season to taste with salt and pepper. Heat chowder until steaming; stir in butter, if desired. Ladle into deep bowls and sprinkle bacon over each portion. Makes 8 servings.

Per serving: 282 calories, 10 g protein, 41 g carbohydrates, 10 g total fat, 25 mg cholesterol, 506 mg sodium

Carrot & Cilantro Soup

Pictured on facing page

Preparation time: About 10 minutes
Cooking time: About 25 minutes

Flavorful bursts of curry and cilantro accent the natural sweetness of carrots in this tantalizing soup. Pair it with Golden Onion & Ham Sandwiches (page 61) for a winning combination.

- 1½ **pounds carrots, peeled**
- 4 **cups regular-strength chicken broth**
- ¾ **teaspoon curry powder**
- 2 **tablespoons lemon juice**
  Ground red pepper (cayenne)
- ¼ **cup lightly packed chopped fresh cilantro (coriander)**

1 Cut carrots into ½-inch-thick slices and place in a 3- to 4-quart pan. Add broth and curry powder and bring to a boil over high heat; reduce heat, cover, and simmer until carrots are very soft (about 20 minutes). Stir in lemon juice.

2 In a blender or food processor, whirl soup, a portion at a time, until puréed. Season to taste with ground red pepper. Ladle soup into bowls and sprinkle cilantro over each portion. Makes 4 servings.

Per serving: 102 calories, 4 g protein, 18 g carbohydrates, 3 g total fat, 0 mg cholesterol, 1,059 mg sodium

Roasted Garlic & Eggplant Soup

Preparation time: About 15 minutes
Cooking time: About 12 minutes

A marvelous first course to be followed by lamb chops and roasted potatoes, this soup showcases the musky eggplant, accented by a hint of mellowed garlic.

- 1 **large eggplant (about 1¼ lbs.), peeled**
  About ¼ cup olive oil or salad oil
- 3 **or 4 cloves garlic, peeled**
- ½ **cup whipping cream**
- 2½ **cups regular-strength chicken broth**
  Salt and pepper
- ¼ **cup chopped parsley**

1 Cut eggplant crosswise into ¾-inch-thick slices. Brush liberally with oil and place in a single layer on a large baking sheet. Broil 4 inches below heat, turning once, until eggplant is soft and browned on both sides (about 10 minutes total).

2 Meanwhile, cook garlic in a small, uncoated frying pan over high heat, turning as needed, until charred all over (about 10 minutes).

3 Cut eggplant into chunks. In a blender or food processor, whirl eggplant, garlic, and cream until puréed. Add broth and whirl until smooth.

4 Transfer soup to a 3- to 4-quart pan and stir over medium heat just until hot. Season to taste with salt and pepper. Ladle soup into bowls and sprinkle parsley over each portion. Makes 4 servings.

Per serving: 262 calories, 3 g protein, 10 g carbohydrates, 24 g total fat, 33 mg cholesterol, 644 mg sodium

In brisk autumn weather, warm up with a bowl of
Carrot & Cilantro Soup (recipe on facing page) and, to
nibble alongside, Golden Onion & Ham Sandwiches
(recipe on page 61).

19

Oriental Noodle & Pea Broth

Preparation time: About 10 minutes
Cooking time: About 7 minutes

Star anise and ginger infuse this light, fresh soup with Asian flavor. Serve the soup with Stir-fried Shrimp with Green Onions (page 72) to carry out the theme.

- ■ ¼ **pound sugar snap peas or Chinese pea pods (snow or sugar peas), ends and strings removed**
- ■ 6 **cups regular-strength chicken broth**
- ■ 2 **whole star anise; or ¼ teaspoon crushed anise seeds and 2 cinnamon sticks (broken into pieces), tied in a cheesecloth bag**
- ■ ¾ **teaspoon grated fresh ginger**
- ■ 1 **ounce thin dry pasta strands, such as spaghettini or vermicelli**

1 Cut peas diagonally into ¼- to ½-inch-thick pieces; set aside.

2 In a 4- to 5-quart pan, bring broth, star anise, and ginger to a boil over high heat. Add pasta; return to a boil and cook, uncovered, just until al dente (about 3 minutes or according to package directions).

3 With a slotted spoon, remove star anise and discard. Add peas and return to a boil. Ladle soup into bowls. Makes 4 to 6 servings.

Per serving: 61 calories, 3 g protein, 8 g carbohydrates, 2 g total fat, 0 mg cholesterol, 1,005 mg sodium

Italian Tomato-Basil Soup

Preparation time: About 10 minutes
Cooking time: 12 to 17 minutes

Celebrate summer with this exquisite soup made with tomatoes and fresh basil. Then, for the main course, offer grilled chicken breasts, crusty bread, and salad.

- ■ 2 **pounds ripe pear-shaped tomatoes**
- ■ 2 **tablespoons olive oil or salad oil**
- ■ ½ **cup lightly packed fresh basil leaves**
- ■ ½ **cup *each* regular-strength chicken broth and whipping cream**
  Salt and pepper

1 Core tomatoes and cut into chunks. Place in a 3- to 4-quart pan with oil and ¼ cup of the basil. Cook, stirring, over medium-high heat until tomatoes mash easily (10 to 15 minutes).

2 In a blender or food processor, whirl tomato mixture, broth, and cream, a portion at a time, until puréed. Season to taste with salt and pepper.

3 Return soup to pan and stir over medium heat just until hot. Ladle soup into bowls. Sliver remaining basil and sprinkle over each portion. Makes 4 servings.

Per serving: 196 calories, 3 g protein, 12 g carbohydrates, 17 g total fat, 33 mg cholesterol, 153 mg sodium

Cold Cucumber
& Dill Soup

Preparation time: About 12 minutes

Cool, crisp cucumbers contrast with delicate pink shrimp in this easy, no-cook soup. For a perfect summertime menu, follow it with cracked crab or lobster.

- **2 large European-style cucumbers (about 1 lb. *each*), peeled**
- **1 cup regular-strength chicken broth**
- **1 cup plain yogurt**
- **¼ cup lightly packed chopped fresh dill**
- **3 tablespoons lime juice**
  Salt
- **½ pound small cooked shrimp**
  Dill sprigs (optional)

1 Cut cucumbers into 1½-inch chunks. Place in a blender or food processor with broth and whirl until puréed.

2 Add yogurt, chopped dill, and lime juice; whirl until blended. Season to taste with salt. (For a smoother texture, rub soup through a fine sieve.)

3 Ladle soup into bowls and top with shrimp. Garnish each portion with dill sprigs, if desired. Makes 4 servings.

Per serving: 131 calories, 17 g protein, 12 g carbohydrates, 2 g total fat, 114 mg cholesterol, 433 mg sodium

Cold Avocado
Soup

Preparation time: About 7 minutes

As a foil for this cool, velvety avocado soup, also present a butter lettuce salad with sliced oranges, onions, and black olives.

- **1 large ripe avocado (about 12 oz.)**
- **½ cup chilled half-and-half or whipping cream**
- **1½ cups regular-strength chicken broth**
- **1 tablespoon lemon juice**
  Salt
  Chopped chives or watercress sprigs (optional)

1 Halve, pit, and peel avocado. In a blender, whirl avocado, half-and-half, broth, and lemon juice until smooth. (To prepare in a food processor, whirl avocado with half-and-half until puréed; add broth and lemon juice and whirl until smooth.) Season to taste with salt.

2 Ladle soup into bowls. Garnish each portion with chives, if desired. Makes 4 servings.

Per serving: 154 calories, 3 g protein, 7 g carbohydrates, 14 g total fat, 11 mg cholesterol, 396 mg sodium

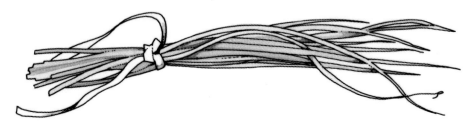

A handful of bold ingredients can quickly become a
simple, yet showy, meal. Warm Spinach & Sausage Salad
(recipe on facing page) is appetizing proof. A splash of
balsamic vinegar and a sprinkling of fennel seeds add
extra bursts of flavor.

Salads

Whether composed of crisp greens with oil and vinegar or a robust blend of meats and vegetables, salads bring refreshment to many different occasions. The following recipes offer a parade of salads at their freshest and most elegant. Choose from gorgeous greens, morsels of seafood, slices of meat, or fresh fruit and vegetables, all treated lightly to simple dressings. Each achieves just the right balance for a tasteful solo performance or menu accompaniment.

Warm Spinach & Sausage Salad

Pictured on facing page

Preparation time: About 15 minutes
Cooking time: About 10 minutes

Not all salads have to be cold or delicate. This substantial combination of spinach, bell pepper, and sausage offers delicious proof. Serve with cheese omelets for brunch, or offer with bread and fruit for dinner.

- ¾ **pound spinach, rinsed well**
- 1 **large red or yellow bell pepper, stemmed and seeded**
- 3 **green onions (including tops)**
- ½ **pound mild or hot Italian sausages, casings removed**
- ½ **teaspoon fennel seeds**
- ⅓ **cup balsamic or red wine vinegar**
  Salt and pepper

1. Remove stems from spinach; tear leaves into pieces. Cut bell pepper lengthwise into thin strips. Cut onions into 3-inch lengths and sliver lengthwise. Place vegetables in a large salad bowl and set aside.

2. In a wide frying pan, cook sausage over medium-high heat, stirring and breaking up with a spoon, until crumbly and browned (about 10 minutes). Add fennel seeds and vinegar, scraping browned bits free.

3. Pour dressing over vegetables and toss well. Season to taste with salt and pepper. Makes 4 to 6 servings.

Per serving: 148 calories, 7 g protein, 3 g carbohydrates, 12 g total fat, 29 mg cholesterol, 310 mg sodium

Japanese Crab & Radish Salad

Pictured on page 3

Preparation time: About 15 minutes

It's quickest to compose this salad by using a food processor, but a sharp knife or mandolin food slicer also works well. Look for the black sesame seeds, if you're using them, in Asian markets. Offer Cold Avocado Soup (page 21) as a prelude to this light main dish.

- 1 **small European-style cucumber (about ½ lb.)**
- 1 **green onion, white and green part separated**
- 10 **medium-size red radishes**
- ½ **to 1 pound crabmeat**
- ⅓ **to ½ cup seasoned rice vinegar**
- 1 **teaspoon toasted black sesame seeds (optional)**

1 Cut cucumber in half crosswise; then cut lengthwise into quarters. Set aside.

2 *To prepare in a food processor*, pack onion (white part only) and as many radishes as will fit into feed tube and slice; repeat to slice remaining radishes. Pack cucumber into feed tube and slice. Remove slicer and spread crabmeat over cucumber. Invert salad onto a large serving platter, spreading out slightly.

To prepare by hand, slice onion (white part only), radishes, and cucumber as thinly as possible. Spread crabmeat on platter and arrange vegetables in layers on top.

3 Pour vinegar over salad. Slice green portion of onion into long, thin strands and scatter over salad; sprinkle with sesame seeds, if desired. Makes 4 servings.

Per serving: 94 calories, 12 g protein, 9 g carbohydrates, 1 g total fat, 57 mg cholesterol, 163 mg sodium

Catalan Avocado & Tomato Platter

Preparation time: About 15 minutes

From northeastern Spain, famous for its robust cuisine, comes this colorful salad. Feature it at a buffet with cold sliced meats, crusty bread, and crisp white wine.

- 2 **medium-size firm-ripe tomatoes, cored**
- 2 **medium-size firm-ripe avocados**
- 12 **large fresh basil leaves**
- 1 **small can (2 oz.) anchovy fillets, drained**
- 3 **tablespoons balsamic or red wine vinegar**
- 1 **tablespoon olive oil**
- ½ **teaspoon pepper**

1 Cut each tomato into 6 equal-size wedges. Pit, peel, and quarter each avocado; set 2 pieces aside. On a serving platter, arrange tomatoes, basil leaves, and remaining avocados.

2 In a blender or food processor, whirl reserved avocado with anchovies, vinegar, oil, and pepper until smooth.

3 Transfer dressing to a small bowl and offer with vegetables. Makes 4 to 6 servings.

Per serving: 157 calories, 4 g protein, 8 g carbohydrates, 13 g total fat, 4 mg cholesterol, 286 mg sodium

Stir-fried Napa Cabbage Salad

Preparation time: About 10 minutes
Cooking time: 2 to 3 minutes

Taking its cue from pickled vegetable dishes popular in Asia, this salad blends wilted napa cabbage with a tart-sweet dressing. Enjoy it in partnership with brown rice or a stir-fry for a nutritious meal.

- 2 tablespoons unseasoned rice vinegar or white wine vinegar
- 2 tablespoons sugar
- 1 tablespoon soy sauce
- ¼ teaspoon ground red pepper (cayenne)
- 1 medium-size head napa cabbage (about 1¼ lbs.)
- 3 tablespoons salad oil

1 Stir together vinegar, sugar, soy sauce, and ground red pepper; set aside.

2 Rinse cabbage, discarding any wilted outer leaves. Cut off base and slice cabbage in half lengthwise. Coarsely chop leaves.

3 Place a wide frying pan or wok over high heat; add oil. When oil is hot, add cabbage and cook, stirring, until it begins to wilt (2 to 3 minutes). Add vinegar mixture, stir well, and remove from heat. Transfer salad to a serving dish. Makes 4 to 6 servings.

Per serving: 94 calories, 1 g protein, 8 g carbohydrates, 7 g total fat, 0 mg cholesterol, 180 mg sodium

Chicken & Pear Salad with Mint

Preparation time: About 20 minutes
Steeping time: 16 to 18 minutes

Crisp pears and a mint dressing lend refreshing contrast to steeped chicken breasts in this main-dish salad. Offer with toasted baguette slices and iced lemon tea for a light lunch or dinner.

- 1 whole chicken breast (about 1 lb.), split
- ½ cup unseasoned rice vinegar or white wine vinegar
- 1½ tablespoons sugar
- 3 tablespoons chopped fresh mint leaves
- 4 to 6 lettuce leaves, washed and dried
- 2 large firm-ripe pears
  Mint sprigs (optional)

1 In a 3- to 4-quart pan, bring 8 cups water to a boil over high heat. Add chicken, pushing into water to cover completely. Cover pan and remove from heat; let chicken steep until no longer pink in thickest part when cut (16 to 18 minutes).

2 Meanwhile, in a small bowl, stir together vinegar, sugar, and chopped mint until sugar is dissolved. Line 2 dinner plates with lettuce leaves; set aside.

3 Lift out chicken and plunge into ice water; drain. Discard skin and bones; cut meat diagonally into thin slices. Peel pears, if desired, and slice thinly. Arrange chicken and pears on lettuce and spoon dressing over. Garnish with mint sprigs, if desired. Makes 2 servings.

Per serving: 349 calories, 35 g protein, 43 g carbohydrates, 4 g total fat, 91 mg cholesterol, 76 mg sodium

Radicchio Cups
with Shrimp & Dill

Pictured on facing page

Preparation time: About 15 minutes
Cooking time: About 5 minutes

Here, just a few luxurious ingredients, artfully arranged, make a light lunch or supper. Round out the menu with rolls and minted iced tea.

- 1 head radicchio (4 to 5 inches in diameter)
- 1 to 2 tablespoons slivered Black Forest, Westphalian, or prosciutto ham
- ⅓ cup olive oil or salad oil
- 1 pound small cooked shrimp
- 2 tablespoons red wine vinegar
- 1½ tablespoons chopped fresh dill or 2½ teaspoons dill weed
  Salt and pepper
  Fresh dill sprigs (optional)

1 Remove 4 large outer leaves from radicchio (reserve remainder for other uses). Rinse leaves, wrap in paper towels, and refrigerate.

2 In a small frying pan, warm ham and oil, stirring over low heat until oil picks up ham flavor (about 5 minutes). Transfer to a medium-size bowl, stirring until cool. Stir in shrimp, vinegar, and chopped dill. Season to taste with salt and pepper.

3 Place a radicchio leaf on each of 4 dinner plates. Spoon shrimp mixture equally into center of each leaf. Garnish with dill sprigs, if desired. Makes 4 servings.

Per serving: 279 calories, 25 g protein, 1 g carbohydrates, 19 g total fat, 223 mg cholesterol, 291 mg sodium

Watermelon-Mint
Salad

Preparation time: About 15 minutes

Crisp, sweet watermelon adopts a new character when mixed with mild onion, cool mint, and a mellow chili dressing. Serve it to complete a summer menu of grilled meat or chicken.

- 1 watermelon (about 6 lbs.)
- ¾ cup slivered mild white onion
- ½ cup minced fresh mint leaves
- 3 tablespoons cider vinegar
- 1 teaspoon chili powder
- 6 tablespoons salad oil
  Salt

1 Slice watermelon into 1-inch-thick rounds; remove and discard rind. Cut flesh into 1-inch cubes, removing visible seeds. Place cubes in a large serving bowl.

2 Add onion and mint to watermelon; mix gently.

3 In a small bowl, whisk together vinegar, chili powder, and oil. Pour dressing over salad and mix to coat well. Season to taste with salt. Makes 8 servings.

Per serving: 155 calories, 1 g protein, 14 g carbohydrates, 11 g total fat, 0 mg cholesterol, 7 mg sodium

Elegant dining is only minutes away when you
feature Radicchio Cups with Shrimp & Dill (recipe on
facing page) on the menu. All you need add are rolls
from the bakery and minted iced tea.

Green Bean & Jicama Salad

Preparation time: About 25 minutes
Cooking time: 3 to 4 minutes

The authoritative crunch in this salad comes from crisp green beans, red onion, and jicama. Enjoy it with fried chicken or sandwiches for a breezy picnic, at home or afield.

- 5 tablespoons white wine vinegar
- ⅔ cup thinly slivered red onion
- ¾ pound green beans, ends trimmed
- 1 pound jicama, peeled
- ⅓ cup olive oil or salad oil
- 2 teaspoons Dijon mustard
  Salt and pepper

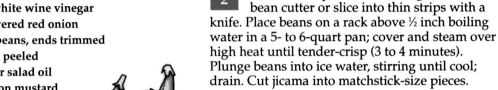

1 In a small bowl, combine 1½ cups cold water with 2 tablespoons of the vinegar. Add onion and let stand for 20 minutes.

2 Meanwhile, pull beans through a French bean cutter or slice into thin strips with a knife. Place beans on a rack above ½ inch boiling water in a 5- to 6-quart pan; cover and steam over high heat until tender-crisp (3 to 4 minutes). Plunge beans into ice water, stirring until cool; drain. Cut jicama into matchstick-size pieces.

3 In a large salad bowl, whisk together oil, mustard, and remaining 3 tablespoons vinegar. Drain onion and add to dressing with beans and jicama; mix to coat well. Season to taste with salt and pepper. Makes 6 to 8 servings.

Per serving: 119 calories, 2 g protein, 9 g carbohydrates, 9 g total fat, 0 mg cholesterol, 43 mg sodium

Carrot Salad with Peppercorns

Pictured on page 67

Preparation time: About 15 minutes
Cooking time: About 2 minutes

Choose cool carrot salad instead of a hot vegetable for your next side dish. Zesty with tarragon and green peppercorns, it sparkles alongside sautéed fish and parsley-strewn rice.

- 4 large carrots (about 1¼ lbs. *total*), peeled
- 2 tablespoons chopped fresh tarragon or 2 teaspoons dry tarragon
- 2 tablespoons canned green peppercorns, drained
- ¼ cup olive oil or salad oil
- 2 tablespoons lemon juice
  Salt and pepper

1 Cut carrots into matchstick-size pieces. (Or cut with julienne blade in a food processor.)

2 In a 3- to 4-quart pan, bring 6 cups water to a boil over high heat. Add carrots and cook, uncovered, until tender-crisp (about 2 minutes). Drain and plunge into ice water, stirring until cool. Drain again.

3 Place carrots, tarragon, peppercorns, oil, and lemon juice in a serving bowl and mix gently. Season to taste with salt and pepper. Makes 4 servings.

Per serving: 186 calories, 2 g protein, 16 g carbohydrates, 14 g total fat, 0 mg cholesterol, 48 mg sodium

Greens Plus

Pictured on page 59

Preparation time: About 10 minutes
Cooking time: 3 to 5 minutes

Starting with a simple green salad, you can create exciting variations. This version, embellished with nuts and oranges and tossed in a delicate dressing, enhances light pasta entrées, poultry, and fish.

- ■ 2 **heads butter lettuce, washed and dried**
- ■ 3 **tablespoons pine nuts or slivered almonds**
- ■ 2 **large oranges**
- ■ ¼ **cup unseasoned rice wine vinegar**
- ■ 1 **tablespoon salad oil**
- ■ ½ **teaspoon dry basil**

1 Tear lettuce into bite-size pieces and place in a large salad bowl.

2 In a small frying pan, toast nuts over low heat, shaking pan often, until golden (3 to 5 minutes). Let cool.

3 With a sharp knife, cut away peel and white membrane from oranges. Separate into segments. Add oranges and nuts to lettuce and toss.

4 In a small bowl, whisk together vinegar, oil, and basil; pour over salad and toss well. Makes 4 servings.

Per serving: 124 calories, 3 g protein, 15 g carbohydrates, 7 g total fat, 0 mg cholesterol, 7 mg sodium

Cherry Tomatoes & Onions Vinaigrette

Preparation time: About 15 minutes

As a change of pace from the standard green salad, a good tomato and onion salad is always welcome. Pungent with garlic and oregano, this one relies on the year-round supply of cherry tomatoes and perks up any casual menu.

- ■ ¼ **cup olive oil or salad oil**
- ■ ⅓ **cup red wine vinegar**
- ■ 1 **small clove garlic, minced or pressed**
- ■ 1 **tablespoon finely chopped fresh oregano leaves or 1 teaspoon dry oregano leaves**
- ■ 7 **to 8 cups cherry tomatoes, stemmed and halved**
- ■ 1 **medium-size mild white onion, thinly sliced**
  Salt and pepper

1 In a large salad bowl, whisk together oil, vinegar, garlic, and oregano.

2 Place tomatoes and onion in bowl with dressing and mix gently to coat well. Season to taste with salt and pepper. Makes 6 to 8 servings.

Per serving: 82 calories, 1 g protein, 5 g carbohydrates, 7 g total fat, 0 mg cholesterol, 7 mg sodium

Subtly seasoned with olive oil and pepper, strands
of squash and pasta swirl through the rich egg
sauce of Spaghetti with Zucchini Carbonara
(recipe on facing page).

Pasta & Eggs

Featuring pasta or eggs as a tempting main course fits right in with today's preference for light and easy cuisine. With the recipes in this chapter, you can have a spectacular dish on the table in no time.

It's easy to prepare a simple, fresh sauce while you're waiting for the pasta water to boil. Equally effortless, the protein-packed egg can be baked, boiled, scrambled, or poached and then eloquently seasoned and presented as a praiseworthy entrée. So, on any night, relax and enjoy the versatility of pasta or eggs.

Spaghetti with Zucchini Carbonara
Pictured on facing page

Preparation time: About 10 minutes
Cooking time: About 20 minutes

We've taken the bacon out of this Italian pasta classic and substituted zucchini. The result is a light, protein-rich—yet meatless—meal of superb flavor. Follow it with Pear Fans with Orange Syrup (page 93).

- 5 tablespoons olive oil or salad oil
- 1 large onion, chopped
- 1 pound zucchini, cut into long, thin strips
- 1 pound spaghetti, linguine, or other dry pasta noodles
- 4 eggs, lightly beaten
- 1 cup (about 5 oz.) shredded or grated Parmesan cheese
  Coarsely ground black pepper

1. In an 8- to 10-quart pan, bring 6 quarts water to a boil over high heat.

2. Meanwhile, heat oil in a wide 3- to 4-quart pan over medium-high heat. Add onion and cook, stirring often, until soft (about 5 minutes). Add zucchini and cook, stirring often, until zucchini is tender (about 8 more minutes).

3. Cook pasta in boiling water until al dente (7 to 9 minutes or according to package directions). Drain. Add noodles and eggs to vegetables. Reduce heat to low and toss until eggs cling to noodles and look slightly scrambled. Add cheese and season to taste with pepper. Toss again. Serve on warm plates. Makes 4 to 6 servings.

Per serving: 559 calories, 24 g protein, 62 g carbohydrates, 23 g total fat, 201 mg cholesterol, 490 mg sodium

Fettucine Gorgonzola

Preparation time: About 7 minutes
Cooking time: 15 to 23 minutes

If you love blue cheese, you won't want to miss this elegant celebration of Gorgonzola, the blue-veined cheese of Italy. Hearty and rich, it needs only a light salad as accompaniment.

- **6 ounces Gorgonzola cheese**
- **1½ cups whipping cream**
- **¼ cup butter or margarine**
- **10 ounces fresh or dry spinach fettucine**
- **⅓ cup grated Parmesan cheese**

1 In an 8- to 10-quart pan, bring 6 quarts water to a boil over high heat. Meanwhile, crumble Gorgonzola; set aside ⅓ cup. In a medium-size frying pan, cook cream, butter, and remaining Gorgonzola over low heat, stirring with a whisk, until smooth (about 3 minutes). Keep warm.

2 Cook noodles in boiling water until al dente (3 to 4 minutes for fresh, 7 to 9 minutes for dry). Drain. Place in a warm bowl, add sauce and Parmesan, and toss until sauce is slightly thickened. Transfer to warm plates. Sprinkle each portion with reserved Gorgonzola. Makes 4 servings.

Per serving: 811 calories, 24 g protein, 54 g carbohydrates, 56 g total fat, 234 mg cholesterol, 771 mg sodium

Pasta Amatriciana

Preparation time: About 10 minutes
Cooking time: About 20 minutes

Savory morsels of bacon and onion add emphasis to a peppery tomato sauce traditionally served over long, hollow noodles called bucatini (or use spaghetti). For a classic Italian feast, accompany with warm garlic bread and red wine.

- **4 slices thick-cut bacon, chopped**
- **1 large onion, chopped**
- **½ teaspoon crushed red pepper flakes**
- **1 large can (28 oz.) pear-shaped tomatoes**
- **1 pound bucatini, spaghetti, or other dry pasta noodles**
- **Grated Parmesan cheese**

1 In an 8- to 10-quart pan, bring 6 quarts water to a boil over high heat. Meanwhile, cook bacon in a wide frying pan over medium-high heat, stirring often, just until fat is rendered (about 3 minutes). Add onion and cook, stirring, until limp (about 7 more minutes). Stir in red pepper flakes.

2 Add tomatoes (break up with a spoon) and their liquid to bacon mixture. Bring to a boil; reduce heat and simmer, stirring occasionally, until slightly thickened (about 10 more minutes).

3 Meanwhile, cook pasta in boiling water until al dente (7 to 9 minutes or according to package directions). Drain. Place pasta in a warm bowl, add tomato sauce, and toss well. Serve on warm plates. Offer cheese to add to taste. Makes 4 to 6 servings.

Per serving: 420 calories, 13 g protein, 65 g carbohydrates, 12 g total fat, 13 mg cholesterol, 347 mg sodium

Pasta Bandiera

Preparation time: About 10 minutes
Cooking time: About 27 minutes

Display the colors of Italy's flag in this delightful red, white, and green seafood pasta. Serve with a green salad and the wine used in the sauce.

- **6 tablespoons butter or margarine**
- **2 large red bell peppers (about ½ lb. *each*), stemmed, seeded, and thinly sliced lengthwise**
- **1 pound scallops, rinsed and dried, cut into quarters if large**
- **2 cups dry white wine**
- **1½ cups whipping cream**
- **8 ounces fresh or dry spinach noodles**

1 In a 6- to 8-quart pan, bring 3 quarts water to a boil over high heat. Meanwhile, melt 3 tablespoons of the butter in a wide frying pan over medium-high heat. Add bell peppers and cook, stirring often, until limp (about 7 minutes). Remove from pan and set aside.

2 Melt remaining 3 tablespoons butter in pan. Add scallops and cook, stirring, until opaque in center when cut (about 1 minute). Remove from pan and set aside. Pour in wine and boil, uncovered, until reduced by half (about 12 minutes). Stir in cream and boil, stirring often, until reduced by about a third (about 7 minutes).

3 Meanwhile, cook noodles in boiling water until al dente (3 to 4 minutes for fresh, 7 to 9 minutes for dry). Drain. Place in a warm bowl. Add sauce, peppers, and scallops; toss well. Serve on warm plates. Makes 4 servings.

Per serving: 762 calories, 30 g protein, 51 g carbohydrates, 49 g total fat, 237 mg cholesterol, 400 mg sodium

Fettucine Emmenthaler

Preparation time: About 7 minutes
Cooking time: 3 to 8 minutes

Rediscover the classic of the 1950s, macaroni and cheese, in this up-to-date version made with fresh pasta and Emmenthaler cheese. Complete a surprisingly sophisticated menu with steamed asparagus and red wine.

- **10 ounces fresh fettucine or dry egg noodles**
- **½ cup (¼ lb.) butter or margarine, melted**
- **2 cups (8 oz.) shredded Emmenthaler or Swiss cheese**
  Freshly ground black pepper
- **¼ cup chopped parsley**

1 In an 8- to 10-quart pan, cook noodles in 6 quarts boiling water until al dente (3 to 4 minutes for fresh, 6 to 7 minutes for dry). Drain. Place noodles in a warm bowl.

2 Immediately add butter and 1 cup of the cheese, rapidly lifting pasta with 2 forks to blend in cheese. Sprinkle with remaining cheese, a little at a time, lifting pasta to mix well. Transfer to warm plates. Sprinkle each portion with pepper and parsley. Makes 4 servings.

Per serving: 693 calories, 26 g protein, 53 g carbohydrates, 42 g total fat, 181 mg cholesterol, 387 mg sodium

Linguine with Prosciutto & Olives

Pictured on facing page

Preparation time: About 10 minutes
Cooking time: 7 to 9 minutes

An assertive combination of prosciutto, onions, and olives complements tender linguine. Offer sliced avocados drizzled with vinaigrette as a smooth foil.

- 8 ounces linguine, spaghetti, or other dry pasta noodles
- 2 ounces thinly sliced prosciutto, cut into ¼-inch-wide strips
- ¼ cup olive oil
- ½ cup thinly sliced green onions (including tops)
- 1 small jar (3 oz.) pimento-stuffed green olives, drained
- 1 cup cherry tomatoes, halved
  Grated Parmesan cheese (optional)

1. In a 6- to 8-quart pan, cook pasta in 3 quarts boiling water until al dente (7 to 9 minutes or according to package directions). Drain. Place pasta in a warm bowl.

2. Meanwhile, combine prosciutto and oil in a wide frying pan. Cook, stirring, over medium-high heat until prosciutto is lightly browned (about 3 minutes). Add onions and cook, stirring, until limp (about 2 more minutes). Add olives and tomatoes and cook, shaking pan often, until olives are hot (about 2 more minutes).

3. Pour prosciutto mixture over noodles and toss well. Transfer to a warm serving bowl. Offer cheese to add to taste, if desired. Makes 2 to 4 servings.

Per serving: 387 calories, 10 g protein, 45 g carbohydrates, 18 g total fat, 8 mg cholesterol, 798 mg sodium

Capellini with Parsley

Preparation time: About 10 minutes
Cooking time: 5 to 7 minutes

Here's proof positive that the best dishes are often the simplest, such as delicate noodles tossed in an incomparable parsley-butter sauce. For a heartier entrée, add slivered cooked ham or chicken to the sauce. For a colorful companion, offer Cherry Tomatoes & Onions Vinaigrette (page 29).

- 8 ounces capellini, vermicelli, or other thin dry pasta
- ⅓ cup butter or margarine
- 1 cup *each* minced parsley and thinly sliced green onions (including tops)
- 2 cloves garlic, minced or pressed
  Salt and coarsely ground black pepper
- Grated Parmesan cheese

1. In a 6- to 8-quart pan, cook pasta in 3 quarts boiling water until al dente (5 to 7 minutes or according to package directions). Drain. Place noodles in a warm bowl.

2. Meanwhile, melt butter in a wide frying pan over medium-low heat. Add parsley, onions, and garlic and cook, stirring, until onions are limp (about 1 minute).

3. Pour parsley sauce over noodles and toss. Season to taste with salt and pepper. Serve on warm plates. Offer cheese to add to taste. Makes 2 servings.

Per serving: 714 calories, 16 g protein, 91 g carbohydrates, 32 g total fat, 82 mg cholesterol, 326 mg sodium

Toss together Linguine with Prosciutto & Olives
(recipe on facing page) for a spectacular Italian entrée
that takes just minutes to create and needs only rustic
bread and Chianti as accompaniments.

Fusilli with Broccoli & Ricotta

Preparation time: About 10 minutes
Cooking time: About 10 minutes

Corkscrew twirls of pasta and spears of tender-crisp broccoli, both coated with creamy ricotta, produce an unforgettable feast. Offer salt-sprinkled breadsticks, a crisp white wine, and fresh fruit to round out the meal.

- 1 **pound broccoli**
- 2 **tablespoons olive oil**
- 5 **green onions (including tops), thinly sliced**
  Coarsely ground black pepper
- 12 **ounces fusilli (corkscrews) or other dry pasta shapes**
- 1½ **cups part-skim ricotta cheese**
- **Grated Parmesan cheese**

1 In an 8- to 10-quart pan, bring 6 quarts water to a boil over high heat. Meanwhile, trim broccoli, leaving about 2 inches of stem below flowerets. Cut lengthwise into spears.

2 Heat oil in a wide frying pan over medium-high heat. Add onions and cook, stirring often, for 1 minute. Add broccoli and cook, stirring often, until broccoli turns bright green (about 3 more minutes).

3 Add ¼ cup water to pan and bring to a boil; reduce heat, cover, and simmer until broccoli is tender-crisp (4 to 6 minutes). Remove from heat. Season to taste with pepper.

4 Meanwhile, cook pasta in boiling water until al dente (7 to 9 minutes or according to package directions). Drain. Place pasta in a warm bowl. Add broccoli mixture and ricotta; toss until blended. Serve on warm plates. Offer cheese to add to taste. Makes 4 servings.

Per serving: 537 calories, 25 g protein, 76 g carbohydrates, 15 g total fat, 29 mg cholesterol, 148 mg sodium

Cold Lemon Noodles

Preparation time: About 12 minutes
Cooking time: 5 to 7 minutes

An echo of the Orient flavors this cool, refreshing pasta. Serve with colorful stir-fried vegetables, either cooked at home or purchased.

- 6 **ounces buckwheat noodles, vermicelli, or other thin dry pasta**
- ¼ **cup lemon juice**
- 2 **tablespoons soy sauce**
- 2 **teaspoons *each* sesame oil and finely chopped fresh ginger**
- ¼ **cup minced fresh cilantro (coriander) or parsley**

1 In a 6- to 8-quart pan, cook noodles in 3 quarts boiling water until al dente (5 to 7 minutes or according to package directions). Drain noodles and rinse with cold water until cool; drain again. Place in a large bowl.

2 In a small bowl, stir together lemon juice, soy sauce, sesame oil, and ginger; pour over noodles. Add cilantro and toss. Serve on chilled plates. Makes 2 servings.

Per serving: 372 calories, 12 g protein, 68 g carbohydrates, 6 g total fat, 0 mg cholesterol, 1,038 mg sodium

Add-on Risotto

Like pasta dishes, risotto is a culinary masterpiece from Italy that begins with a nutritious but ordinary starch (rice, in this case) and transforms it into an elegant first course or entrée. Start with the basic recipe below; then dress it up in a variety of ways by adding extra ingredients. We suggest three possibilities, but you can create a repertoire of add-on risottos by using seafood, meat, chopped herbs, cheese, or cooked vegetables.

For best results, use imported arborio rice (look for it in Italian markets and specialty food stores); domestic short- or long-grain rice also works.

Basic Risotto

- 3½ cups regular-strength chicken broth (if salted, use half broth and half water)
- 3 tablespoons butter or margarine
- 1 medium-size onion, chopped
- 1 cup arborio, short-grain, or long-grain white rice
- About ¼ cup grated Parmesan cheese

1 In a small pan, bring broth to a simmer over medium heat; reduce heat to low.

2 In a 2- to 3-quart pan, melt butter over medium heat. Add onion and cook, stirring, until soft (about 5 minutes). Add rice and stir until opaque and well coated with butter (about 2 more minutes).

3 Add ½ cup of the broth to rice and cook, stirring, until absorbed. Continue to cook, adding broth ½ cup at a time and stirring constantly after each addition until absorbed, until rice is just tender but not starchy (20 to 25 minutes).

4 Remove from heat and stir in cheese; let stand for 2 minutes. Serve in warm bowls. Makes 4 servings.

Per serving: 288 calories, 6 g protein, 40 g carbohydrates, 11 g total fat, 27 mg cholesterol, 623 mg sodium

Saffron Risotto
Pictured on page 38

Follow directions for **Basic Risotto** (above), adding a large pinch of **saffron threads** or ⅛ teaspoon saffron powder to broth as it heats. Makes 4 servings.

Risotto with Asparagus

Snap off tough ends from ½ pound **asparagus** and cut spears into ½-inch lengths. Drop into boiling water to cover and cook until barely tender (about 3 minutes). Drain.

Follow directions for **Basic Risotto** (above), adding asparagus to rice with last addition of broth. Makes 4 servings.

Risotto with Roasted Red Pepper

Cut 1 large **red bell pepper** into quarters; discard stem and seeds. Broil, skin sides up, 2 or 3 inches below heat until blackened (about 5 minutes). Peel off skin under cold water. Cut into ½-inch squares.

Follow directions for **Basic Risotto** (above), adding bell pepper to rice with last addition of broth. Makes 4 servings.

Popular in Milan as a first course, often followed by
veal, creamy Saffron Risotto (recipe on page 37) is
subtle in flavor and vibrant in color.

Mozzarella Carriages

Preparation time: About 7 minutes
Cooking time: About 8 minutes

A popular first course in Italy, these egg-dipped sandwiches also make a thrifty and appetizing entrée. If you wish, top each serving with heated spaghetti sauce.

- ■ **4 thick slices mozzarella cheese (about 4 oz. *total*)**
- ■ **8 slices French bread, crusts removed**
- ■ **¾ cup milk**
- ■ **⅓ cup all-purpose flour**
- ■ **2 eggs, lightly beaten with 1 tablespoon water**
- ■ **About 3 tablespoons butter or margarine**
  Lemon wedges (optional)

1 Trim cheese, if necessary, so slices are just slightly smaller than bread. Make 4 sandwiches, using 2 slices of the bread and 1 slice of the cheese for each. Place milk, flour, and egg mixture in separate shallow dishes.

2 In a wide frying pan, melt 2 tablespoons of the butter over medium-high heat. Quickly coat 2 of the sandwiches, 1 at a time, first with milk, then flour, and then eggs. Place immediately in pan and cook, turning once, until golden brown and crusty on both sides (about 4 minutes total). Repeat with remaining sandwiches, adding butter to pan as needed. Transfer sandwiches to warm plates. Offer with lemon, if desired. Makes 4 servings.

Per serving: 392 calories, 15 g protein, 36 g carbohydrates, 21 g total fat, 190 mg cholesterol, 514 mg sodium

Hangtown Fry

Preparation time: About 30 minutes
Cooking time: About 7 minutes

Popular during California's Gold Rush days, this quick supper satisfied a suddenly rich miner's extravagant tastes. It's still a treat today, especially when accompanied with a smooth Chardonnay and a loaf of sourdough bread.

- ■ **5 eggs**
- ■ **2 tablespoons whipping cream**
- ■ **¼ pound shucked raw oysters, drained**
- ■ **All-purpose flour**
- ■ **3 tablespoons cracker crumbs**
- ■ **3 tablespoons butter or margarine**
  Salt and pepper

1 Beat eggs with cream until blended; set aside. Rinse oysters and pat dry. Coat with flour, shaking off excess. Dip in egg mixture, roll in crumbs, and place slightly apart on a rack; let stand until slightly dry (about 20 minutes).

2 In a wide frying pan, melt 2 tablespoons of the butter over medium-high heat. When butter is hot, add oysters and cook, turning once, until golden (about 2 minutes total). Lift out and set aside on paper towels.

3 Melt remaining 1 tablespoon butter in pan and pour in remaining egg mixture. Cook, lifting edges with a spatula to let uncooked portion flow underneath, until eggs are set but still moist on top (about 5 minutes). Slide onto a warm platter and top with oysters. Season to taste with salt and pepper. Makes 2 to 4 servings.

Per serving: 235 calories, 10 g protein, 6 g carbohydrates, 19 g total fat, 390 mg cholesterol, 221 mg sodium

Eggs & Tomatoes
Italian

Preparation time: About 12 minutes
Cooking time: About 11 minutes

This one-pan egg and vegetable bake is a colorful choice for a casual supper. Excellent with cooked ham, it also goes well with steamed green beans for a meatless menu.

- **4 large firm-ripe tomatoes**
- **3 tablespoons butter or margarine**
- **1 pound mushrooms, sliced**
- **8 eggs**
  Salt and pepper
- **¾ cup shredded jack cheese**
- **1 tablespoon chopped fresh oregano leaves or parsley**

1 Immerse tomatoes in boiling water to cover for 10 seconds; lift out and slip off skins. Core, cut into cubes, and let drain in a colander.

2 Meanwhile, melt butter in a wide frying pan over medium heat. Add mushrooms and cook, stirring, until soft (about 7 minutes). Add tomatoes, stirring until hot.

3 Spread vegetables evenly in pan; with back of a spoon, make 8 depressions and break an egg into each. Season to taste with salt and pepper; top with cheese. Reduce heat, cover, and simmer until eggs are set to your liking (3 to 4 minutes for firm whites and soft yolks). Sprinkle with oregano and serve from pan. Makes 4 servings.

Per serving: 371 calories, 21 g protein, 13 g carbohydrates, 27 g total fat, 590 mg cholesterol, 356 mg sodium

Egg & Asparagus
Gratins

Preparation time: About 7 minutes
Cooking time: 16 to 18 minutes

Parmesan-dusted eggs join asparagus in light, individual servings that are both attractive and appetizing. Accompany with tomatoes vinaigrette and toasted brioche or rolls.

- **12 asparagus spears, tough ends removed**
- **4 tablespoons butter or margarine**
- **8 eggs**
- **½ cup grated Parmesan cheese**

1 In a wide frying pan, bring 2 inches water to a boil over high heat. Add asparagus, reduce heat, and simmer, uncovered, until tender (about 5 minutes). Drain.

2 Meanwhile, place 1 tablespoon of the butter in each of 4 small ovenproof dishes. Set dishes on a baking sheet and place in a 450° oven just until butter is melted (about 5 minutes).

3 Remove dishes from oven and quickly lay 3 asparagus spears in each. Carefully break 2 eggs into each dish, return to oven, and bake until set to your liking (5 to 7 minutes for firm whites and soft yolks). Sprinkle with cheese and bake for 1 more minute. Makes 4 servings.

Per serving: 315 calories, 18 g protein, 3 g carbohydrates, 26 g total fat, 587 mg cholesterol, 442 mg sodium

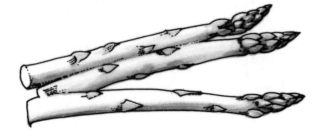

Country Omelet

Preparation time: About 10 minutes
Cooking time: About 14 minutes

Strewn with peas and bacon, this omelet is served open-faced. Pair it with fried potatoes for an informal supper.

- 4 slices bacon, cut into 1-inch pieces
- About 2 tablespoons butter or margarine, melted
- 8 eggs, lightly beaten
- 1 cup frozen tiny peas, thawed
- 1 cup (4 oz.) shredded Swiss cheese
- Freshly grated or ground nutmeg

1. In a wide ovenproof frying pan, cook bacon, stirring often, over medium-high heat until crisp (about 7 minutes). Lift out, drain on paper towels, and set aside. Measure pan drippings and add enough butter to make ¼ cup total.

2. Return drippings and butter to pan and reduce heat to medium-low. Pour in eggs and cook, lifting edges with a spatula to let uncooked portion flow underneath, until set but still moist on top (about 5 minutes). Halfway through cooking, sprinkle peas over eggs.

3. Remove from heat, scatter bacon in center, and sprinkle with cheese. Broil about 4 inches below heat until cheese is melted (about 2 minutes). Dust with nutmeg. Cut into wedges and serve from pan. Makes 4 servings.

Per serving: 472 calories, 24 g protein, 8 g carbohydrates, 38 g total fat, 605 mg cholesterol, 489 mg sodium

Potato Frittata

Preparation time: About 10 minutes
Cooking time: 20 to 25 minutes

An unfolded omelet, a frittata makes an attractive company entrée, sliced into wedges and served with Italian Tomato-Basil Soup (page 20). To give it its characteristic browning, this frittata is finished under the broiler for extra ease.

- 4 eggs
- 2 tablespoons milk
- 2 tablespoons butter or margarine
- 1 medium-size russet potato (about ½ lb.), thinly sliced
- 3 green onions (including tops), thinly sliced

1. Beat eggs with milk until blended; set aside. In a wide ovenproof frying pan, melt butter over medium heat; tilt pan to coat bottom and sides. Add potato, cover, and cook, turning, until tender (12 to 15 minutes). Uncover, increase heat to medium-high, and cook until lightly browned (about 5 more minutes). Sprinkle with onions.

2. Pour in egg mixture and cook, lifting edges with a spatula to let uncooked portion flow underneath, until set around edge (2 to 3 minutes). Broil about 4 inches below heat until puffed and golden (about 2 minutes). Cut into wedges and serve from pan. Makes 2 to 4 servings.

Per serving: 183 calories, 8 g protein, 12 g carbohydrates, 12 g total fat, 291 mg cholesterol, 136 mg sodium

Zucchini-Basil Omelet for Two

Pictured on facing page

Preparation time: About 10 minutes
Cooking time: About 12 minutes

Dinner-for-two is ready in no time with this generous omelet that boasts a sunny filling of zucchini, tomatoes, and basil. Alongside, offer warm pita bread and fresh fruit. (For best results, prepare the omelet in a nonstick pan.)

- 4 **tablespoons butter or margarine**
- 2 **medium-size zucchini (about ½ lb.** *total***), diced**
  Coarsely ground black pepper
- ¼ **cup chopped fresh basil leaves**
- 5 **eggs, lightly beaten with 2 tablespoons water**
- 3 **ounces shredded jack cheese**
- ¼ **cup canned crushed tomatoes**

1 In a 2- to 3-quart pan, melt 2 tablespoons of the butter over medium-high heat. Add zucchini and cook, stirring often, just until crisp (about 3 minutes). Season to taste with pepper. Reduce heat, cover, and simmer until tender (about 5 more minutes). Stir in basil and set aside.

2 In a 12-inch frying pan, melt remaining 2 tablespoons butter over medium-high heat; tilt pan to coat bottom and sides. Pour in eggs and cook, lifting edges with a spatula to let uncooked portion flow underneath, until set but still moist on top (about 4 minutes).

3 Sprinkle cheese over half of omelet and top with zucchini and tomatoes. Remove from heat, loosen from pan, and slide onto a large platter, flipping untopped portion over filling. Cut in half and transfer to warm plates. Makes 2 servings.

Per serving: 587 calories, 28 g protein, 8 g carbohydrates, 50 g total fat, 784 mg cholesterol, 688 mg sodium

Gingered Eggs & Tomatoes

Preparation time: About 10 minutes
Cooking time: About 5 minutes

Adding a hint of the Orient to scrambled eggs transforms this breakfast standby into a savory stir-fry. Offer with Cold Lemon Noodles (page 36).

- 2 **tablespoons salad oil**
- 3 **eggs, lightly beaten**
- 1 **tablespoon slivered fresh ginger**
- 2 **green onions (including tops), thinly sliced**
- 2 **large firm-ripe tomatoes, cored and cut into ½-inch wedges**
  Soy sauce

1 Place a wok or wide frying pan over medium heat. When pan is hot, add oil. When oil is hot, add eggs and cook, lifting edges with a spatula to let uncooked portion flow underneath, until set (about 2 minutes). Break eggs into small pieces.

2 Add ginger and onions and cook, stirring, until eggs are dark golden (about 2 more minutes). Add tomatoes, stirring until hot. Season to taste with soy sauce. Transfer eggs to a warm serving bowl. Makes 2 servings.

Per serving: 273 calories, 11 g protein, 9 g carbohydrates, 22 g total fat, 411 mg cholesterol, 116 mg sodium

Oversize Zucchini-Basil Omelet for Two (recipe on facing page) cuts preparation time in half. Complete a relaxed and casual supper with pita wedges and slices of fresh fruit.

Unbeatable Breakfasts

If you love breakfast but you'd rather jog in the park or stay in bed than spend a lot of time cooking it, outsmart the clock by relying on the following breakfast spectaculars.

Simplify pancakes by baking a Dutch Baby instead. Warm risotto cereal and an egg and ham brunch all come together in a snap. Or blend lox and cream cheese into one-pan scrambled eggs. Even bacon needs less attention when baked in the oven. With all these shortcuts, there's no excuse to skip breakfast anymore.

Tender Dutch Baby

- 3 eggs
- 6 tablespoons all-purpose flour
- 1 tablespoon granulated sugar
- 6 tablespoons milk
- 3 tablespoons butter or margarine
- Powdered sugar
- Lemon wedges (optional)

1 In a blender or food processor, whirl eggs, flour, granulated sugar, and milk until smooth, scraping edges of container as needed.

2 Place butter in a 10- to 12-inch ovenproof frying pan and set on a rack slightly above center in a 425° oven. When butter is melted (about 4 minutes), remove pan and tilt to coat bottom and sides. Quickly pour in batter, return pan to oven, and bake until pancake is puffed and golden brown (about 15 minutes).

3 Sprinkle with powdered sugar and cut into wedges. If desired, offer lemon to squeeze over individual portions. Makes 6 servings.

Per serving: 146 calories, 4 g protein, 12 g carbohydrates, 9 g total fat, 155 mg cholesterol, 101 mg sodium

Spiced Risotto Cereal

- 4 tablespoons butter or margarine
- 1½ cups long-grain white rice
- 4⅓ cups water
- 1½ cups milk
- 1 teaspoon anise seeds
- ½ cup sugar
- 1 teaspoon ground coriander

1 In a 4- to 5-quart pan, melt 2 tablespoons of the butter over medium heat. Add rice and cook, stirring, until opaque (about 2 minutes).

2 Add water and milk and bring to a boil over high heat; reduce heat and simmer, uncovered, stirring occasionally at first and more often when liquid is almost absorbed, until rice is tender but still creamy (20 to 30 minutes).

3 Meanwhile, lightly crush anise seeds with back of a spoon or a mortar and pestle. Mix with sugar and coriander.

4 When rice is cooked, stir in ¼ cup of the anise mixture. Ladle into warm bowls and offer remaining anise mixture and butter to add to taste. Makes 6 to 8 servings.

Per serving: 256 calories, 4 g protein, 43 g carbohydrates, 8 g total fat, 23 mg cholesterol, 85 mg sodium

Ham, Egg & Asparagus Brunch

- 4 large slices sourdough or French bread
- 6 tablespoons olive oil
- 1 medium-size onion, thinly sliced
- 1 pound asparagus, tough ends removed
- ½ pound cooked ham, cut into thin strips
- 4 eggs

1 Lightly brush both sides of bread with 2 tablespoons of the oil. In a wide frying pan, toast bread over medium-high heat, turning once, until browned on both sides (about 5 minutes total). Place a slice on each of 4 dinner plates; keep warm.

2 Add 2 more tablespoons of the oil to pan with onion, asparagus, and ham. Cook, stirring often, until asparagus is tender (5 to 7 minutes). Evenly spoon asparagus mixture beside bread on each plate.

3 Add remaining 2 tablespoons oil to pan and tilt to coat. Break eggs into pan and fry until done to your liking (about 2 minutes for firm whites and soft yolks). Place an egg atop asparagus mixture on each plate. Makes 4 servings.

Per serving: 461 calories, 24 g protein, 20 g carbohydrates, 32 g total fat, 308 mg cholesterol, 1,086 mg sodium

Cream Cheese Eggs with Smoked Salmon

- 6 eggs
- 4 ounces thinly sliced smoked salmon or lox, cut into thin strips
- 1 green onion (including top), thinly sliced
- 1 tablespoon butter or margarine
- 1 small package (3 oz.) cream cheese, cut into small pieces

1 Beat eggs until blended; stir in salmon and half the onion.

2 In a wide frying pan, melt butter over medium heat. Pour in egg mixture and cook, stirring often, until eggs are set but still moist on top (about 5 minutes). Scatter cheese over eggs and continue to cook, stirring often, until set to your liking. Spoon onto warm plates and garnish with remaining onion. Makes 4 servings.

Per serving: 252 calories, 16 g protein, 2 g carbohydrates, 20 g total fat, 449 mg cholesterol, 418 mg sodium

Sugared Bacon Twists

- 12 slices bacon
- 3 tablespoons firmly packed brown sugar

1 Line a large baking pan with foil and lay bacon slices, side by side, on foil. Bake in a 350° oven for 10 minutes. Remove from pan and drain off fat.

2 Evenly sprinkle bacon with sugar, smoothing with back of a spoon to spread sugar evenly. Return to pan and continue to bake until golden brown (about 12 more minutes).

3 Transfer to a wire rack. Protecting your hands with oven mitts or foil, crisscross 2 bacon slices, pinch in center, and twist in opposite directions. Repeat to make 6 twists total. Let cool for 5 minutes. Makes 6 servings.

Per serving: 94 calories, 4 g protein, 6 g carbohydrates, 6 g total fat, 11 mg cholesterol, 204 mg sodium

Grilled to tantalizing succulence and surrounded by
fresh herbs, Pounded Veal Chops with Lemon &
Thyme (recipe on facing page) are as easy on the cook
as a summer breeze.

Meats

Do you love the rich, robust flavor of meat—but not the fuss of a complex roast or stew? By choosing such tender cuts as loins, chops, and ground meats, you can achieve mouth-watering taste with minimal seasoning and quick cooking methods.

For elegance, choose sautéed meat with a pan sauce; or go casual with a stir-fry. Pan-fry or grill to produce succulent results with ultimate ease. Each time, you'll turn out meat to savor without having to spend all day at it.

Pounded Veal Chops with Lemon & Thyme

Pictured on facing page

Preparation time: About 15 minutes
Grilling time: 4 to 5 minutes

Rubbed with a fragrant blend of herbs and lemon, pounded thin, then grilled on a hot fire, these chops present a chorus of summer pleasures. Keep the menu simple by using the barbecue to prepare Grilled Vegetables (page 69) as well.

- 3 tablespoons minced fresh thyme leaves or 1½ tablespoons dry thyme leaves
- 2 teaspoons grated lemon peel
- ½ cup minced parsley
- 2 tablespoons olive oil or salad oil
- 4 veal rib or loin chops (about 1¼ lbs. *total*), cut ¾ to 1 inch thick
  Thyme sprigs (optional)
- Lemon wedges

1. Stir together minced thyme, lemon peel, parsley, and oil. Slash connective tissue around edge of each chop at 1-inch intervals. Rub each side with about 1½ teaspoons of the thyme mixture.

2. Place chops between sheets of plastic wrap and pound meat until ¼ inch thick.

3. Place meat on a greased grill about 6 inches above a solid bed of glowing coals and grill, turning once, until done to your liking (4 to 5 minutes total for medium). Transfer to a warm serving platter and garnish with thyme sprigs, if desired. Offer lemon wedges to squeeze over individual portions. Makes 4 servings.

Per serving: 193 calories, 19 g protein, 2 g carbohydrates, 12 g total fat, 95 mg cholesterol, 80 mg sodium

Veal Chops Milanese

Preparation time: About 15 minutes
Cooking time: 8 to 12 minutes

Crispy outside and juicy inside, this classic Italian veal dish needs only crusty bread and red wine to enhance it. Offer any version of risotto (page 37) as a first course and finish with purchased gelato.

- ■ 6 boneless veal chops (about 1½ lbs. *total*), cut ¾ to 1 inch thick
- ■ About ⅓ cup all-purpose flour
  Salt and pepper
- ■ 3 eggs, well beaten
- ■ About 1 cup seasoned fine dry bread crumbs
- ■ About 4 tablespoons butter or margarine
- ■ About 4 tablespoons salad oil
  Lemon wedges (optional)

1 Slash connective tissue around edge of each chop at 1-inch intervals. Pound chops between sheets of plastic wrap until ¼ inch thick.

2 Dredge chops in flour, shaking off excess; season to taste with salt and pepper. Dip each chop in beaten eggs, drain briefly, and turn in crumbs until well coated, pressing in crumbs so they adhere. Set chops aside.

3 Heat 1 tablespoon *each* of the butter and oil in a wide frying pan over medium-high heat. Add chops, a portion at a time, and cook, turning once, until golden brown outside and just slightly pink in center when cut (about 4 minutes total); add more oil and butter as needed. Transfer to warm plates. Offer lemon to squeeze over individual portions, if desired. Makes 6 servings.

Per serving: 433 calories, 35 g protein, 19 g carbohydrates, 23 g total fat, 292 mg cholesterol, 699 mg sodium

Roast Ribs

Preparation time: About 5 minutes
Baking time: 25 to 30 minutes

Here's a hands-on rib feast without the messy sauce. Succulent beef ribs, roasted to perfection with herbs and seasonings, need nothing more. Have your butcher prepare the ribs in large sections for even cooking. Flanked by corn on the cob and french fries, they make a no-utensil meal.

- ■ 8 pounds beef standing rib bones
- ■ 2 teaspoons *each* dry rosemary, dry thyme leaves, and rubbed sage
  Salt and pepper

1 Arrange ribs in a single layer on racks in 2 large roasting pans, overlapping to fit, if necessary.

2 In a small bowl, combine rosemary, thyme, and sage; rub evenly over ribs. Season to taste with salt and pepper.

3 Roast in a 500° oven until meat between ribs is done to your liking when cut (25 minutes for rare, 30 minutes for medium). Transfer ribs to large serving platters; slice between bones. Makes 8 servings.

Per serving: 733 calories, 41 g protein, 1 g carbohydrates, 62 g total fat, 161 mg cholesterol, 120 mg sodium

Pan-fried Steaks
with Vermouth Glaze

Preparation time: About 5 minutes
Cooking time: 10 to 14 minutes

Sometimes, nothing hits the spot as well as a juicy steak. Finished with a smooth glaze of mustard and vermouth, it tastes even better. Risotto-style Corn (page 80) and buttered noodles bring appetizing contrast to the menu.

- 1 tablespoon butter or margarine
- 1 tablespoon salad oil
- 4 boneless top sirloin or New York strip steaks (about 2 lbs. *total*), cut 1 to 1½ inches thick
- 1 tablespoon Dijon mustard
- 3 tablespoons dry vermouth or dry white wine

 1 Heat butter and oil in a wide frying pan over medium-high heat. Add steaks and cook, turning once, until browned outside and still pink in center when cut (10 to 14 minutes total). Transfer to warm plates and set aside.

2 Add mustard and vermouth to pan drippings and stir briskly until hot. Spoon sauce over steaks. Makes 4 servings.

Per serving: 460 calories, 49 g protein, 2 g carbohydrates, 27 g total fat, 144 mg cholesterol, 256 mg sodium

San Francisco
Burgers

Preparation time: About 7 minutes
Cooking time: About 11 minutes

When you're hankering for hamburgers, try this special recipe, inspired by San Francisco's Chinatown. French fries alongside are traditional, but lightly sprinkle them with crushed red pepper flakes for an unusual twist.

- 1½ pounds lean ground beef
- Salad oil
- Purchased oyster sauce
- 4 thick slices sourdough or French bread
- Dijon mustard
- 4 large butter lettuce leaves, washed and dried

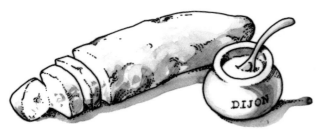

1 Shape beef into 4 equal-size patties about ¾ inch thick. Lightly coat a wide frying pan with oil; set over medium-high heat. When pan is hot, add patties and cook, turning once, until done to your liking (about 10 minutes total for medium-rare). Remove patties and discard fat.

2 Spread a side of each patty with about ½ tablespoon of the oyster sauce; return patties to pan, sauce sides down, and cook just until glazed (about 30 seconds). Spread tops of patties with same amount of sauce; turn and cook for 30 more seconds.

3 Lightly toast bread slices and place on plates. Spread each slice with 1 teaspoon of the mustard and 2 teaspoons of the oyster sauce. Top with a lettuce leaf and a patty. Offer additional mustard and oyster sauce to add to taste. Makes 4 servings.

Per serving: 482 calories, 36 g protein, 27 g carbohydrates, 25 g total fat, 104 mg cholesterol, 1,056 mg sodium

Pork Tenderloins with Stilton & Port

Pictured on facing page

Preparation time: About 7 minutes
Cooking time: About 19 minutes

Two classic partners—Stilton cheese and port—join in the sauce for this elegant rendition of roasted pork. Jalapeño peppers add a bold garnish (or leave them out for a milder result). Sautéed Peppers & Pears (page 80) enhance this dish especially well.

- 1 tablespoon salad oil
- 2 or 3 pork tenderloins (1½ lbs. *total*), trimmed of fat
- 1 cup port
- ½ cup regular-strength chicken broth
- ½ cup whipping cream
- ¼ pound Stilton cheese, crumbled
- 1 or 2 fresh jalapeño chiles, halved lengthwise, stemmed, seeded, and diced (optional)

1 Heat oil in a wide frying pan over medium-high heat. Add pork and cook, turning, until browned (about 4 minutes total). Transfer meat to a baking pan and bake in a 400° oven until a meat thermometer inserted in thickest part registers 160° (about 15 minutes).

2 Meanwhile, discard fat from frying pan and add port and broth. Boil over high heat until reduced to about ¾ cup (about 3 minutes). Stir in cream and continue to boil, stirring, until large, shiny bubbles form (about 5 more minutes). Add cheese and stir until melted; stir in jalapeños, if desired. Remove from heat.

3 Slice meat thinly across grain. Fan slices on warm plates and spoon sauce over meat. Makes 4 to 6 servings.

Per serving: 294 calories, 29 g protein, 6 g carbohydrates, 17 g total fat, 110 mg cholesterol, 414 mg sodium

Baked Pork Chops Dijon

Preparation time: About 7 minutes
Baking time: 18 to 20 minutes

Baked with a tart mustard dressing, these pork chops stay moist and tender. A hearty entrée, it goes well with Spiced Spinach & Potatoes (page 85) and a Merlot wine.

- 6 loin pork chops (about 2½ lbs. *total*), cut ¾ inch thick
- 6 tablespoons olive oil or salad oil
- ¼ cup red wine vinegar
- 2 tablespoons Dijon mustard
- 1 tablespoon minced chives
- 1 teaspoon dry tarragon
  Freshly ground black pepper

1 Arrange chops in a foil-lined rimmed baking pan. Set aside.

2 In a small bowl, whisk together oil, vinegar, mustard, chives, and tarragon. Season to taste with pepper.

3 Spread 1 tablespoon of the baste over each chop. Bake on upper rack of a 475° oven for 10 minutes. Turn and spread each with 1 more tablespoon of the baste; bake until no longer pink in center when cut (8 to 10 more minutes). Transfer to warm plates. Makes 6 servings.

Per serving: 401 calories, 28 g protein, 1 g carbohydrates, 31 g total fat, 101 mg cholesterol, 146 mg sodium

Expecting guests for dinner? Slices of Pork
Tenderloins with Stilton & Port (recipe on facing
page) are artfully arranged with Sautéed Peppers
& Pears (recipe on page 80) for a stunning
company presentation.

Stir-fried Pork with Green Onions

Preparation time: About 10 minutes
Cooking time: 4 to 6 minutes

For quick cooking and fresh flavor, stir-frying is hard to beat. Taste this medley of pork and onions to judge for yourself. Also offer steamed rice and sesame oil–sprinkled vegetables to carry through the Asian theme.

- ½ **pound boneless pork, such as loin or shoulder**
- 1 **tablespoon cornstarch**
- 1 **tablespoon rice wine or dry sherry**
- 2 **tablespoons salad oil**
- ½ **pound green onions (including tops), cut into slivers**
- 3 **cloves garlic, minced or pressed**
  Salt and pepper

1 Cut meat across grain into thin slices; then cut lengthwise into matchstick-size strips. In a small bowl, combine cornstarch and wine; add pork, stirring to coat well.

2 Set a wok or wide frying pan over high heat. When pan is hot, add oil and swirl to coat bottom. When oil is hot, add pork mixture and cook, stirring, until lightly browned (2 to 3 minutes). Add onions and garlic and continue to cook, stirring, for 2 to 3 more minutes. Spoon into a warm serving bowl. Season to taste with salt and pepper. Makes 2 servings.

Per serving: 486 calories, 23 g protein, 12 g carbohydrates, 38 g total fat, 79 mg cholesterol, 70 mg sodium

Sausage & Fig Grill

Preparation time: About 10 minutes
Grilling time: About 15 minutes

In this all-grill menu, spicy sausages cook alongside herbed bread and skewers of cheese and fresh figs (available in early summer and again in fall). To cool the palate, offer white wine spritzers with fresh mint.

- 4 **or 8 hot or mild Italian sausages**
- ¼ **cup butter or margarine, melted**
- 1 **tablespoon fresh rosemary or 1 teaspoon dry rosemary**
- 8 **thin slices French bread**
- 12 **small or 6 large fresh figs, stems trimmed**
- 6 **ounces Jarlsberg cheese, cut into 1-inch chunks**

1 Place sausages on a grill about 6 inches above a solid bed of hot coals and grill, turning often, until meat is no longer pink in center when cut (about 15 minutes).

2 Meanwhile, stir together butter and rosemary. Brush bread with some of the mixture and grill, turning once, until toasted on both sides (about 5 minutes total). Set aside.

3 Cut large figs, if used, in half. Alternate figs and cheese on each of 4 skewers. Grill, turning once and basting with remaining butter mixture, until figs are warm and cheese is soft (2 to 4 minutes).

4 Transfer skewers to a warm serving platter and accompany with toast and sausages. Makes 4 servings.

Per serving: 774 calories, 33 g protein, 57 g carbohydrates, 44 g total fat, 111 mg cholesterol, 1,400 mg sodium

Lamb-stuffed Celery

Preparation time: About 10 minutes
Baking time: About 25 minutes

Baked celery stalks, filled with garlicky ground lamb, present an innovative and savory dinner entrée. Serve on a platter with brown rice or a bulgur wheat pilaf.

- 1½ **pounds ground lamb**
- 4 **cloves garlic, minced or pressed**
- 2 **eggs**
- ¼ **cup finely chopped fresh mint leaves or 1 tablespoon dry mint**
  Salt and pepper
- 8 **to 10 large celery stalks**
- **Prepared horseradish or mustard**

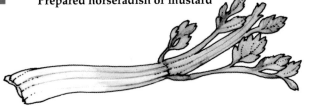

1 With a fork, blend together lamb, garlic, eggs, and mint. Season to taste with salt and pepper. Set aside.

2 Cut leaves from celery and reserve for garnish (use leaves from inner stalks, if necessary). With a vegetable peeler, remove tough strings from celery. Rinse and pat dry.

3 Pack ⅓ to ½ cup of the meat mixture, mounding slightly, in hollow of each stalk. Arrange, meat sides up, slightly apart in a large baking pan. Bake in a 400° oven until meat is browned (about 25 minutes).

4 Arrange stalks on a warm serving platter with leaves at one end. Offer horseradish to add to each portion. Makes 4 or 5 servings.

Per serving: 399 calories, 26 g protein, 5 g carbohydrates, 30 g total fat, 210 mg cholesterol, 171 mg sodium

---

Pounded Lamb Chops with Rosemary

Preparation time: About 15 minutes
Grilling time: About 4 minutes

Garlic, herbs, and olive oil lavish these lamb chops with robust flavor. Pounding works the seasonings into the meat, as well as reduces the grilling time. Skewer your favorite vegetables to barbecue alongside.

- 4 **cloves garlic, minced or pressed**
- 2 **tablespoons minced fresh rosemary or 1 tablespoon crumbled dry rosemary**
- ½ **cup minced parsley**
- 2 **tablespoons olive oil or salad oil**
- 4 **lamb rib or loin chops (about 1¼ lbs. *total*), cut ¾ to 1 inch thick**
  Fresh rosemary sprigs (optional)

1 Stir together garlic, minced rosemary, parsley, and oil. Slash fat around edge of each chop at 1-inch intervals. Rub each side of chops with about 1 tablespoon of the rosemary mixture.

2 Place chops between sheets of plastic wrap and pound meat until ¼ inch thick.

3 Place meat on a greased grill about 6 inches above a solid bed of glowing coals and grill, turning once, until done to your liking (about 4 minutes total for medium-rare). Transfer to warm plates and garnish with rosemary sprigs, if desired. Makes 4 servings.

Per serving: 201 calories, 19 g protein, 2 g carbohydrates, 13 g total fat, 58 mg cholesterol, 55 mg sodium

Aromatic with rosemary and garlic, Game Hens with
Mustard Crust (recipe on facing page) offer
magnificent eating for amazingly little effort.

Poultry

Versatile poultry is one of the most practical choices for dinner. Chicken's mild flavor works well as a background for subtle to bold seasonings. Breast meat especially appeals to time-conscious cooks, since it needs little more than a quick sauté or brief baking.

Other birds work magic in the pan or oven as well. Plump game hens and turkey breasts and fillets offer welcome variety when poultry's on the menu for dinner, as it often is.

Game Hens with Mustard Crust

Pictured on facing page

Preparation time: About 12 minutes
Baking time: 25 to 30 minutes

Cloaked in mustard and herbs, these small gilded birds make a showy presentation. Put some baking potatoes in the oven about 20 minutes before the game hens; then serve together.

- ¼ **cup butter or margarine, melted**
- ¼ **cup coarse-grained or Dijon mustard**
- 1 **tablespoon minced fresh or crumbled dry rosemary**
- 2 **cloves garlic, minced or pressed**
- 4 **Cornish game hens (about 1¼ lbs. each), thawed if frozen**
  Fresh rosemary sprigs (optional)

1. Mix butter, mustard, minced rosemary, and garlic; set aside.

2. Remove necks and giblets from game hens; reserve for other uses, if desired. With poultry shears or a sharp knife, cut hens lengthwise along each side of backbone and remove bone. Spread hens open; place, skin sides up, on a flat surface and press down firmly on hens to flatten (bones will crack). Rinse hens, pat dry, and coat both sides with mustard mixture. Set slightly apart on 2 large baking sheets.

3. Bake in a 450° oven until meat near thighbone is no longer pink when cut (25 to 30 minutes). Cut hens in half lengthwise through breastbone, if desired. Transfer to a warm serving platter and garnish with rosemary sprigs, if desired. Makes 4 servings.

Per serving: 718 calories, 69 g protein, 2 g carbohydrates, 47 g total fat, 251 mg cholesterol, 473 mg sodium

Chicken au Poivre

Preparation time: About 10 minutes
Cooking time: 8 to 12 minutes

Sautéing mellows the heat and emphasizes the spiciness of the peppercorns that season these chicken breasts. For an elegant company menu, also offer steamed asparagus and rice pilaf. Choose a zinfandel wine to balance the assertive sauce.

- 3 whole chicken breasts (about 1 lb. *each*), skinned, boned, and split
- 1 tablespoon crushed black or white peppercorns or 3 tablespoons crushed dried pink, green, or Szechwan peppercorns
- 4 to 6 tablespoons butter or margarine
- ¾ cup Madeira or dry sherry
- ¾ cup whipping cream
- ½ teaspoon dry rosemary

1 Pound chicken between sheets of plastic wrap until ¼ inch thick. Sprinkle each side with ¼ teaspoon of the black or white peppercorns, or ¾ teaspoon of others. Lightly pound into meat.

2 In a wide frying pan, melt 2 tablespoons of the butter over high heat. Add chicken, a portion at a time, and cook, turning once, until no longer pink in center when cut (2 to 3 minutes total); add more butter as needed. Transfer to a warm serving platter; keep warm.

3 Add Madeira to pan, scraping to free browned bits. Add cream and rosemary and boil, stirring, until reduced by half (3 to 4 minutes). Spoon over chicken. Makes 6 servings.

Per serving: 335 calories, 35 g protein, 5 g carbohydrates, 19 g total fat, 139 mg cholesterol, 187 mg sodium

Lemon Basil Chicken

Pictured on front cover

Preparation time: About 10 minutes
Cooking time: About 15 minutes

Basil-brightened pan juices, enriched with butter, become a delectable sauce for sautéed chicken breasts. Serve on a bed of white rice with steamed zucchini for a light, fresh menu.

- ½ cup (¼ lb.) butter or margarine
- 2 whole chicken breasts (about 1 lb. *each*), skinned, boned, and split
- 1 cup regular-strength chicken broth
- 2 teaspoons grated lemon peel
- 2 tablespoons lemon juice
- 3 tablespoons chopped fresh basil leaves or 1 tablespoon dry basil
  Fresh basil leaves (optional)

1 In a wide frying pan, melt 2 tablespoons of the butter over medium-high heat. Add chicken and cook, turning once, until lightly browned (about 4 minutes total). Add broth, lemon peel, and lemon juice. Reduce heat, cover, and simmer until chicken is no longer pink in center when cut (about 5 more minutes). Transfer to a warm serving platter; keep warm.

2 Increase heat to high and boil pan juices until reduced by half (2 to 3 minutes). Reduce heat to medium; pour in any accumulated juices from chicken. Add remaining butter and cook, stirring, until sauce coats back of a spoon.

3 Stir in chopped basil. Pour sauce around chicken and garnish with basil leaves, if desired. Makes 4 servings.

Per serving: 379 calories, 35 g protein, 2 g carbohydrates, 25 g total fat, 148 mg cholesterol, 583 mg sodium

Chicken & Apple Sauté

Preparation time: About 12 minutes
Cooking time: About 20 minutes

Apples and sherry subtly sweeten these tender sautéed chicken breasts. Complete a menu for a crisp fall evening with Bacon Polenta (page 82) and steamed carrots.

- 4 **tablespoons butter or margarine**
- 2 **large tart apples, peeled, cored, and sliced ¼ inch thick**
- 2 **whole chicken breasts (about 1 lb. *each*), boned and split**
- 1 **large onion, chopped**
- ⅔ **cup dry sherry or apple juice**
- ⅓ **cup whipping cream**

1 In a wide frying pan, melt 2 tablespoons of the butter over medium heat. Add apples and cook, stirring often, just until tender (1 to 2 minutes). Lift out and keep warm.

2 Increase heat to medium-high and melt remaining butter in pan. Add chicken and cook, turning once, until golden (about 4 minutes total). Lift out and keep warm.

3 Add onion and cook, stirring, until golden (about 7 minutes). Add sherry; boil for 1 minute. Return chicken to pan, skin sides up. Reduce heat, cover, and simmer until no longer pink in center when cut (about 5 minutes). Transfer to a warm serving platter; top with apples and keep warm. Add cream to pan and boil, stirring, until sauce coats back of a spoon (2 to 3 minutes). Pour over chicken. Makes 4 servings.

Per serving: 396 calories, 35 g protein, 19 g carbohydrates, 20 g total fat, 139 mg cholesterol, 224 mg sodium

Chutney Chicken

Preparation time: About 10 minutes
Baking time: 15 to 18 minutes

Bite into these crisp chicken rolls and encounter the exotic taste of their chutney filling. Hot steamed brown rice and curry-seasoned vegetables round out an Indian-inspired meal.

- 2 **tablespoons light rum**
- 3 **tablespoons butter or margarine, melted**
- **About ⅓ cup fine dry seasoned bread crumbs**
- 3 **whole chicken breasts (about 1 lb. *each*), skinned, boned, and split**
- 1 **jar (9 oz.) Major Grey's chutney, chopped**
- 2 **tablespoons slivered almonds**

1 Combine rum and butter in a shallow dish. Pour crumbs onto wax paper.

2 Lay breasts skinned sides down. Place about 1 tablespoon of the chutney and 1 teaspoon of the almonds in center of each. Fold to enclose. Dip in rum and coat with crumbs. Place, seam sides down, in a baking pan and drizzle with any remaining rum mixture.

3 Bake in a 425° oven until no longer pink in center when cut (15 to 18 minutes). Transfer to warm plates. Offer with any remaining chutney. Makes 6 servings.

Per serving: 341 calories, 34 g protein, 27 g carbohydrates, 9 g total fat, 101 mg cholesterol, 402 mg sodium

Raspberry-glazed
Turkey Tenderloins

Pictured on facing page

Preparation time: About 7 minutes
Cooking time: 10 to 13 minutes

A fruit glaze keeps lean and light turkey breast tenderloins (sometimes called fillets) moist during broiling. Then it doubles as a distinctive sauce. Serve with Greens Plus (page 29) and herb-sprinkled pasta.

- ½ cup seedless raspberry jam
- 6 tablespoons raspberry vinegar
- ¼ cup Dijon mustard
- 1 teaspoon grated orange peel
- ½ teaspoon dry thyme leaves
- 4 turkey breast tenderloins (about 2¼ lbs. *total*)

1 In a 2- to 3-quart pan, whisk together jam, vinegar, mustard, orange peel, and thyme. Bring to a boil over high heat and cook, stirring, until reduced by about a fourth (2 to 3 minutes). Reserving about ½ cup of the glaze, coat turkey with some of the remaining glaze.

2 Set turkey on a rack in a broiler pan. Broil about 4 inches below heat, turning and basting once with remaining glaze, until no longer pink in center when cut (8 to 10 minutes total). Slice crosswise and arrange on warm plates. Offer with reserved glaze. Makes 4 to 6 servings.

Per serving: 281 calories, 40 g protein, 21 g carbohydrates, 3 g total fat, 106 mg cholesterol, 417 mg sodium

Turkey Scaloppine

Preparation time: About 12 minutes
Cooking time: About 12 minutes

Stretch both your budget and your poultry repertoire by trying inexpensive turkey. The breast, sliced and thinly pounded, provides an excellent substitute for veal, as you'll discover when you taste this version of scaloppine. Any risotto on page 37 goes well as a first course.

- 1 pound boned turkey breast, sliced ¼ inch thick
- All-purpose flour
- ½ cup (¼ lb.) butter or margarine
- ½ pound medium-size mushrooms, cleaned and sliced
- ½ cup Marsala
- Lemon wedges and parsley sprigs (optional)

1 Pound turkey between sheets of plastic wrap until ⅛ inch thick. Coat with flour, shaking off excess.

2 In a wide frying pan, melt 2 tablespoons of the butter over medium-high heat. Add turkey, a portion at a time, and cook, turning once, until lightly browned (about 2 minutes total); add more butter as needed. Transfer to a warm serving platter; keep warm.

3 Add mushrooms to pan and cook, stirring, until browned (5 to 7 minutes). Add Marsala, scraping pan to free browned bits. Lift out mushrooms and spoon over turkey. Cook liquid over high heat, stirring, until large, shiny bubbles form (about 1 minute). Stir in remaining butter. Pour over turkey and garnish with lemon and parsley, if desired. Makes 4 servings.

Per serving: 375 calories, 28 g protein, 9 g carbohydrates, 25 g total fat, 132 mg cholesterol, 315 mg sodium

Stage a stylish event by featuring Raspberry-glazed
Turkey Tenderloins (recipe on facing page). In
supporting roles, offer Greens Plus (recipe on page 29)
and herbed pasta bows.

Sandwich Sensations

Easy and portable, sandwiches are naturals for meals of few ingredients. But that doesn't have to mean a slapdash arrangement of cold meats, sliced bread, and condiments. With the recipes that follow you can create hot sandwiches bursting with fresh, vivid flavors. Carried outside to the patio or served indoors, they bring a picnic mood to the table at any time of year.

To round out the menu, choose a soup or salad (pages 15–29) for starters and finish with ice cream or fruit for dessert.

Roasted Red Pepper & Avocado Melts

- 4 whole wheat English muffins
- 8 thin slices red onion
- 1 large ripe avocado
- 8 thin slices jack cheese (about 4 oz. *total*)
- 2 jars (7 oz. *each*) roasted red bell peppers or pimentos, drained
- 3 tablespoons grated Parmesan cheese

1 Split muffins in half and place, cut sides up, on a large baking sheet. Broil about 6 inches below heat until toasted (about 2 minutes).

2 Place 1 slice of the onion on each muffin half. Halve, pit, and peel avocado; slice each half into 8 wedges. Top each onion slice with 2 of the avocado wedges, 1 slice of the jack, and an equal portion of the bell peppers. Sprinkle with Parmesan. Return to oven and broil until jack is melted (2 to 3 minutes). Makes 4 to 8 servings.

Per serving: 187 calories, 7 g protein, 18 g carbohydrates, 10 g total fat, 14 mg cholesterol, 229 mg sodium

Quesadillas

- 1 tablespoon butter or margarine
- 4 flour tortillas (7 inches in diameter)
- 1 cup (4 oz.) grated Cheddar or jack cheese
- ¼ cup *each* thinly sliced green onions (including tops) and chopped fresh cilantro (coriander)

1 In a small frying pan, melt half the butter over medium-high heat. Add a tortilla and cook until soft (about 30 seconds). Sprinkle ¼ cup of the cheese over half the tortilla and top with 1 tablespoon *each* of the onions and cilantro. With tongs, fold tortilla in half.

2 Cook, turning once, until cheese is melted (1 to 2 minutes total); remove and keep warm. Repeat to cook remaining tortillas, adding more butter as needed. Makes 4 servings.

Per serving: 256 calories, 10 g protein, 25 g carbohydrates, 13 g total fat, 38 mg cholesterol, 415 mg sodium

Chicken & Cheese Subs

- 1 whole chicken breast (about 1 lb.), split
- 4 slices bacon
- 4 unsliced French sandwich rolls (*each about 3 by 6 inches*)
- 8 ounces Camembert, fontina, or jack cheese, cut into 16 equal chunks
- 2 tablespoons butter or margarine, melted

1 In a 3- to 4-quart pan, bring 1 quart water to a boil. Add chicken; reduce heat, cover, and simmer until chicken is no longer pink in center when cut (about 15 minutes). Drain, discard skin and bones, and shred meat. Meanwhile, cook bacon in a wide frying pan over medium-high heat until crisp (about 7 minutes); drain.

2 Slice off ends of rolls to expose insides. With a knife, carefully scoop out and discard insides, leaving a ¼-inch-thick shell. Fill each roll with 1 slice of the bacon, 4 chunks of the cheese, and an equal portion of the chicken, using some to plug ends. Lay rolls on a large rimmed baking sheet and brush with butter.

3 Bake in a 450° oven until crisp and browned (6 to 8 minutes). Slice rolls diagonally across center. Makes 4 servings.

Per serving: 545 calories, 36 g protein, 38 g carbohydrates, 27 g total fat, 110 mg cholesterol, 1,072 mg sodium

Golden Onion & Ham Sandwiches

Pictured on page 19

- 4 large onions
- ¼ cup butter or margarine
- 6 slices dark rye bread
  Dijon or German mustard
- 6 thin slices (6 oz. *total*) Black Forest, Westphalian, or baked ham
- 6 slices (about 5 oz. *total*) Swiss cheese
  Coarsely ground black pepper

1 Thinly slice onions and separate into rings. In a wide frying pan, melt butter over medium-high heat. Add onions and cook, stirring occasionally, until very limp and golden (about 25 minutes).

2 About 5 minutes before onions are done, place bread in a single layer on a large baking sheet. Broil about 4 inches below heat, turning once, until toasted (about 2 minutes total). Spread top of each slice with mustard; add 1 slice *each* of the ham and cheese. Return to oven and broil until cheese is melted (about 1 minute). Spoon onions equally on each sandwich. Season to taste with pepper. Makes 6 servings.

Per serving: 286 calories, 15 g protein, 21 g carbohydrates, 16 g total fat, 55 mg cholesterol, 694 mg sodium

Italian Bell Pepper & Sausage Rolls

- 6 mild or hot Italian sausages (about 1¼ lbs. *total*), casings removed
- 1 large onion, thinly sliced
- 2 large green or red bell peppers (or 1 of each), stemmed, seeded, and thinly sliced lengthwise
- ¼ cup butter or margarine, at room temperature
- 6 sandwich rolls (3 to 4 inches in length), split open

1 Place sausages, one at a time, between sheets of plastic wrap and flatten with your hand into thin patties about same length as rolls.

2 In a wide frying pan, cook patties over medium-high heat, turning once, until well browned and no longer pink in center when cut (about 5 minutes total). Lift out and keep warm. Add onion and bell peppers to pan and cook, stirring often, until limp (about 10 minutes). Return sausage patties to pan and cook just until hot (about 2 more minutes).

3 Meanwhile, spread butter on insides of rolls and broil, buttered sides up, about 4 inches below heat until toasted. Put a sausage patty inside each roll and top each patty equally with onion mixture. Makes 6 servings.

Per serving: 610 calories, 20 g protein, 42 g carbohydrates, 40 g total fat, 95 mg cholesterol, 1,166 mg sodium

Vivid tomatoes, hot chile, and zesty cilantro
lend an unmistakably Latin accent to full-flavored fish
in Swordfish Steaks with Salsa (recipe on facing page).

Seafood

More abundant and varied than ever before, fish and shell-fish present such an array of choices that it's fun to feature them often on the menu. It's easy, too, because seafood requires little preparation and cooks quickly. From delicate sole to meaty yellowfin tuna to succulent scallops, there's a taste to suit every palate.

To accent seafood's fresh flavors, the following recipes rely on simple sauces and delicate marinades. For best results, buy fish or shellfish only from reliable fish markets and cook it the same day.

Swordfish Steaks with Salsa

Pictured on facing page

Preparation time: About 12 minutes
Cooking time: About 10 minutes

A vivid sauce of tomatoes, chile, and cilantro lends Mexican zest to pan-fried swordfish. To complete the fiesta, also serve black beans and sliced avocados, topped with sour cream.

- 4 swordfish steaks (about 2 lbs. *total*)
- 2 tablespoons salad oil
- 2 cloves garlic, minced or pressed
- 1 jalapeño or other small hot chile, stemmed, seeded, and minced
- 5 firm-ripe pear-shaped tomatoes, seeded and diced
- ½ cup packed fresh cilantro (coriander) leaves, chopped

1. Rinse fish and pat dry. Heat oil in a wide frying pan over medium-high heat. Add fish and cook, turning once, until well browned and just opaque in center when cut (about 7 minutes total). Transfer to a warm serving platter; keep warm.

2. Add garlic and chile to pan and cook, stirring, until fragrant (about 30 seconds). Add tomatoes and cilantro and cook, stirring, until hot (about 2 more minutes). Spoon over fish. Makes 4 servings.

Per serving: 349 calories, 46 g protein, 3 g carbohydrates, 16 g total fat, 89 mg cholesterol, 209 mg sodium

Sand Dabs
with Basil-Chili Butter

Preparation time: About 10 minutes
Broiling time: About 4 minutes

Junior members of the sole family, sand dabs are cooked whole and boned at the table. Also serve cornbread and sautéed peppers to complement the spicy flavors of this dish.

- ■ ½ cup (¼ lb.) butter or margarine, at room temperature
- ■ 2 teaspoons chili powder
- ■ 2 tablespoons minced fresh basil leaves or 2 teaspoons dry basil
- ■ 4 whole sand dabs (about ½ lb. *each*), cleaned and trimmed, or 1 pound sole fillets
- ■ All-purpose flour
- ■ 2 tablespoons salad oil

1 Mix butter, chili powder, and basil until well blended. Set aside.

2 Rinse fish and pat dry. Dredge in flour, shaking off excess. Heat oil in a large rimmed baking pan about 4 inches below broiler. When oil is hot, add fish, carefully turning to coat, and broil until just opaque in center when cut (about 4 minutes).

3 Transfer fish to warm plates. Top each portion with a dollop of the butter mixture. Makes 4 servings.

Per serving: 372 calories, 22 g protein, 4 g carbohydrates, 30 g total fat, 117 mg cholesterol, 339 mg sodium

Broiled Trout
with Macadamia Butter

Preparation time: About 10 minutes
Broiling time: About 7 minutes

Nuts and trout—a proven combination—take on a delicious new dimension when the nuts are macadamias. Look for boned and butterflied trout (or ask your fishmonger to prepare it). For crispness and color alongside, steam delicate Chinese pea pods, seasoning them with extra nut butter.

- ■ ¼ cup butter or margarine, at room temperature
- ■ 1½ teaspoons brown sugar
- ■ 1 jar (3½ oz.) salted macadamia nuts
- ■ 4 boned trout (about 8 oz. *each*), heads removed
- ■ Freshly ground black pepper
- ■ 1 lemon, quartered

1 In a food processor or blender, whirl butter, half the sugar, and ½ cup of the macadamias until nuts are finely ground. Set aside.

2 Rinse fish and pat dry. Spread open and place, skin sides down, in a single layer in a greased shallow baking pan. Sprinkle with remaining sugar. Season to taste with pepper. Place about 2 teaspoons of the nut mixture on each fish.

3 Broil about 4 inches below heat until butter is soft (about 1 minute). Remove pan and quickly spread butter evenly over fish. Return to broiler and cook until just opaque in thickest part when cut (5 to 6 more minutes). Transfer fish to warm plates and garnish with lemon. Evenly sprinkle with remaining nuts and, if desired, offer remaining nut mixture to spoon on individual portions. Makes 4 servings.

Per serving: 539 calories, 38 g protein, 8 g carbohydrates, 41 g total fat, 130 mg cholesterol, 428 mg sodium

Baby Salmon with Sautéed Leeks

Preparation time: About 20 minutes
Cooking time: About 20 minutes

Buttery leeks, spooned inside butterflied baby salmon (or trout), make a simple, delicately flavored stuffing. Offer with couscous or boiled small new potatoes and a crisp white wine.

- About 1½ pounds leeks
- 4 tablespoons butter or margarine
- ½ teaspoon dry thyme leaves
- 2 tablespoons lemon juice
  Salt and ground white pepper
- 6 boned baby salmon or trout (about 8 oz. *each*), heads removed
  Lemon wedges (optional)

1 Trim and discard root ends and tough green tops from leeks; remove tough outer leaves. Split leeks in half lengthwise and rinse well; slice (you should have about 3 cups).

2 In a wide frying pan, melt 2 tablespoons of the butter over medium heat. Add leeks and cook, stirring, until soft (8 to 10 minutes). Stir in thyme and lemon juice; season to taste with salt and pepper.

3 Rinse fish and pat dry. Spread open and place, skin sides down, in a single layer in a greased baking pan. Spoon leek mixture down center of each fish. Melt remaining 2 tablespoons butter and drizzle over fish. Bake in a 400° oven until just opaque in thickest part when cut (about 10 minutes). Transfer to warm plates and garnish with lemon wedges, if desired. Makes 6 servings.

Per serving: 341 calories, 35 g protein, 7 g carbohydrates, 19 g total fat, 114 mg cholesterol, 164 mg sodium

Broiled Salmon with Sherry-Soy Butter

Preparation time: About 10 minutes
Cooking time: 8 to 11 minutes

Juxtaposing the richness of salmon with bold Oriental seasonings produces delicious contrast. Steamed asparagus completes a beautiful menu.

- 1 tablespoon sesame seeds
- 2 tablespoons butter or margarine
- 2 tablespoons *each* thinly sliced green onions (including tops) and dry sherry
- 1 tablespoon soy sauce
- 4 boned baby salmon (about 8 oz. *each*), heads removed, or 4 salmon fillets or steaks (about 6 oz. *each*)

1 In a small frying pan, toast sesame seeds over medium-low heat, shaking pan often, until golden (2 to 3 minutes). Add butter, onions, sherry, and soy sauce; cook, stirring, until butter is melted. Remove from heat.

2 Rinse fish and pat dry. Place on a greased rack in a large broiler pan (spread baby salmon open and place skin sides down). Brush with butter mixture. Broil about 4 inches below heat until just opaque in thickest part when cut (6 to 8 minutes). Transfer to warm plates. Offer with any remaining sauce. Makes 4 servings.

Per serving: 312 calories, 34 g protein, 2 g carbohydrates, 18 g total fat, 109 mg cholesterol, 392 mg sodium

Ahi with Bacon

Pictured on facing page

Preparation time: About 5 minutes
Cooking time: About 15 minutes

If you've only tasted tuna from a can, treat yourself to meaty ahi, as it's called in Hawaii, seasoned with bacon, soy sauce, and wine. Offer Carrot Salad with Peppercorns (page 28) as a colorful side dish.

- 4 slices bacon
- 4 ahi (yellowfin tuna) steaks (about 1½ lbs. *total*), each about 1 inch thick
- 4 teaspoons butter or margarine
- 2 tablespoons soy sauce
- ½ cup dry white wine

1 In a wide frying pan, cook bacon over medium-high heat until crisp (about 7 minutes). Lift out and drain. Discard all but 1 tablespoon of the drippings from pan.

2 Rinse fish and pat dry. Add to pan, increase heat to high, and cook, turning once, until browned. Dot fish with butter; add soy sauce and wine. Reduce heat to medium, cover, and cook until pale pink in center when cut (about 5 minutes). Transfer to warm plates; keep warm.

3 Boil sauce, uncovered, until reduced to about 3 tablespoons (2 to 3 minutes). Top each steak with sauce and 1 slice of the bacon. Makes 4 servings.

Per serving: 283 calories, 42 g protein, 1 g carbohydrates, 11 g total fat, 95 mg cholesterol, 735 mg sodium

Orange Roughy with Sesame Seeds

Preparation time: About 10 minutes
Baking time: 8 to 10 minutes

A newcomer to our markets, orange roughy is now one of the most popular fish available. Lean and mild, it's a perfect foil for a crunchy sesame coating. Offer Chinese pea pods, sprinkled with sesame oil, and brown rice alongside.

- 1 large egg white
- ⅓ cup sesame seeds
- 4 orange roughy fillets (1½ to 2 lbs. *total*)
- 2 tablespoons salad oil
- Lemon wedges
- Soy sauce

1 Beat egg white in a shallow pan until slightly frothy. Put sesame seeds in another shallow pan. Rinse fish and pat dry. Dip fillets on one side only in egg and drain briefly. Lay egg-moistened side in sesame seeds, coating heavily. Lay fillets, seed sides up, on wax paper.

2 Heat a large baking pan in a 500° oven for 5 minutes. Add oil, swirling to coat, and then add fish, seed sides down, in a single layer. Bake until fish is just opaque in thickest part when cut (8 to 10 minutes).

3 Transfer fillets, seed sides up, to warm plates. Offer lemon and soy sauce to add to taste. Makes 4 servings.

Per serving: 347 calories, 28 g protein, 3 g carbohydrates, 25 g total fat, 34 mg cholesterol, 121 mg sodium

Taste a seafood celebrity from Hawaii, fresh yellowfin
tuna, in Ahi with Bacon (recipe on facing page). For
appetizing color alongside, also serve Carrot Salad
with Peppercorns (recipe on page 28).

Breezy Grilling

The oldest cooking method known to man, grilling is still one of the easiest. Though many foods grill well, here we spotlight two that barbecue quickly and taste superb without marinating—tender beef and fish steaks. For an extra fillip of flavor, take a few minutes to whip up a seasoned butter that melts enticingly on the cooked steaks. And use the barbecue to grill some vegetables as well.

For these recipes, start the fire about 20 minutes before you plan to cook. Use enough charcoal to cover the grate in a solid bed, and burn it until it's slightly covered with gray ash and you can hold your hand over the grill only 2 or 3 seconds.

Grilled Beef Steaks

Pictured on page 70

Cilantro-Chili Butter or Horseradish Butter (recipes at right), optional
- 4 tender steaks (6 to 8 oz. *each*), such as boneless top sirloin or T-bone; or 1½ to 2 pounds top round (London broil), cut 2 inches thick

Salt and pepper

1 Prepare flavored butter of your choice, if desired. Set aside.

2 Place meat on a grill 4 to 6 inches above a solid bed of hot coals. Grill, turning once, until meat is well browned and a thermometer inserted in center registers 140° for rare (10 to 12 minutes total for individual steaks, 24 to 30 minutes total for thick steak).

3 Season to taste with salt and pepper. Cut top round (if used) across grain into thin strips. Place on a warm serving platter. Offer flavored butter (if used) to spoon on individual portions. Makes 4 servings.

Per serving: 266 calories, 38 g protein, 0 g carbohydrates, 11 g total fat, 106 mg cholesterol, 75 mg sodium

Grilled Fish Steaks

Pictured on page 70

Dill Butter or Cilantro-Chili Butter (recipes at right), optional
- 4 salmon, tuna, swordfish, halibut, or sturgeon steaks (about 1½ lbs. *total*)
- Olive oil or salad oil

Salt and pepper

1 Prepare flavored butter of your choice, if desired. Set aside.

2 Rinse fish and pat dry. Rub with oil. Place on a grill 4 to 6 inches above a solid bed of hot coals. Grill, turning once or twice, until fish is just opaque (or tuna is slightly pink) in center when cut (6 to 10 minutes total).

3 Transfer fish to a warm serving platter and season to taste with salt and pepper. Offer flavored butter (if used) to spoon on individual portions. Makes 2 to 4 servings.

Per serving: 272 calories, 34 g protein, 0 g carbohydrates, 14 g total fat, 94 mg cholesterol, 75 mg sodium

Grilled Vegetables

Pictured on page 70

- 2 to 4 red or yellow onions
- 2 to 4 crookneck squash, summer squash, or zucchini
- 2 to 4 slender leeks
- 2 to 4 red, yellow, or green bell peppers
- ½ cup olive oil or salad oil
- 2 tablespoons minced fresh oregano leaves, thyme leaves, rosemary, or tarragon; or 2 teaspoons dry herbs
  Salt and pepper

1 Peel onions and cut in half lengthwise. Trim ends off squash and cut in half lengthwise. Trim and discard root ends from leeks, split in half lengthwise, and rinse well. Leave bell peppers whole.

2 In a 4- to 6-quart pan, bring 2 quarts water to a boil over high heat. Add squash and leeks and cook for 2 minutes; drain, plunge into ice water, and drain again.

3 In a small bowl, combine oil and oregano. Brush vegetables all over with oil mixture. Place on a grill 4 to 6 inches above a solid bed of hot coals. Grill, turning and basting often with remaining oil mixture, until tender and streaked with brown (6 to 8 minutes for squash and leeks, 10 to 15 minutes for onions and peppers). Transfer to a warm serving platter. Season to taste with salt and pepper. Makes 6 to 8 servings.

Per serving: 149 calories, 1 g protein, 7 g carbohydrates, 14 g total fat, 0 mg cholesterol, 5 mg sodium

Cilantro-Chili Butter

Pictured on page 70

- ¼ cup butter or margarine, at room temperature
- 1 teaspoon chili powder
- 1 tablespoon minced fresh cilantro (coriander)

1 Mix butter, chili powder, and cilantro until well combined. Transfer to a small serving crock. Makes 4 servings.

Per serving: 104 calories, 0.2 g protein, 0.3 g carbohydrates, 12 g total fat, 31 mg cholesterol, 123 mg sodium

Dill Butter

Pictured on page 70

- ¼ cup butter or margarine, at room temperature
- ¼ cup chopped fresh dill or 2 tablespoons dill weed

1 Mix butter and dill until well combined. Transfer to a small serving crock. Makes 4 servings.

Per serving: 106 calories, 0.4 g protein, 0.8 g carbohydrates, 12 g total fat, 31 mg cholesterol, 120 mg sodium

Horseradish Butter

- ¼ cup butter or margarine, at room temperature
- 1 teaspoon prepared horseradish
- 1 tablespoon Dijon mustard

1 Mix butter, horseradish, and mustard until well combined. Transfer to a small serving crock. Makes 4 servings.

Per serving: 107 calories, 0.1 g protein, 0.6 g carbohydrates, 12 g total fat, 31 mg cholesterol, 231 mg sodium

Hot off the grill! This menu features (from top
to bottom) herb-basted Grilled Vegetables, Grilled
Fish Steaks with Dill Butter, and Grilled Beef Steaks
with Cilantro-Chili Butter. Recipes are on pages 68–69.

Baked Fish
with Tapenade & Tomatoes

Preparation time: About 10 minutes
Baking time: 15 to 20 minutes

Tapenade, an olive and garlic paste traditional in the south of France, anoints mild fish with a burst of pungent flavor. Tomatoes add vibrant color while keeping the cooked fillets moist. Serve with warm, crusty bread and a green salad.

- 4 skinless white-fleshed fish fillets (about 6 oz. *each*), such as halibut, sea bass, or cod
- 5 tablespoons olive oil or salad oil
- 2 medium-size tomatoes, cored and sliced ½ inch thick
- 1 can (6 oz.) pitted ripe olives, drained
- 1 clove garlic

1. Rinse fish and pat dry. Place in a single layer in a shallow baking pan. Brush with 1 tablespoon of the oil; arrange tomatoes over fillets.

2. Bake in a 375° oven until fish is just opaque in thickest part when cut (15 to 20 minutes). Meanwhile, in a food processor or blender, whirl olives and garlic until finely minced. Add remaining 4 tablespoons oil in a thin, steady stream, whirling until mixture forms a paste. Transfer fish to warm plates. Spoon olive mixture evenly over each fillet. Makes 4 servings.

Per serving: 427 calories, 36 g protein, 4 g carbohydrates, 29 g total fat, 54 mg cholesterol, 416 mg sodium

Sea Bass &
Shrimp Provençal

Preparation time: About 15 minutes
Cooking time: About 20 minutes

Tender shrimp bake with white-fleshed sea bass in a garlicky tomato-mushroom sauce. Accompany with steamed broccoli and thick slices of toasted bread.

- 3 medium-size tomatoes, peeled
- 3 tablespoons butter or margarine
- ¼ pound mushrooms, thinly sliced
- 2 cloves garlic, minced or pressed
  Salt and pepper
- 2 pounds sea bass steaks, *each* about 1 inch thick
- ½ pound medium-size raw shrimp, shelled and deveined
  Lemon slices and parsley sprigs (optional)

1. Seed and coarsely chop 2 of the tomatoes. Cut remaining tomato into 6 wedges; set aside.

2. In a medium-size frying pan, melt butter over medium-high heat. Add mushrooms and cook, stirring, until limp (about 5 minutes). Add chopped tomatoes and garlic and cook, stirring, until hot. Season to taste with salt and pepper.

3. Rinse fish and shrimp and pat dry. Place fish in a single layer in a shallow baking pan; top with shrimp. Spoon tomato sauce over seafood.

4. Bake in a 400° oven until fish and shrimp are just opaque in center when cut (about 15 minutes). Transfer to a warm serving platter and surround with tomato wedges. Garnish with lemon and parsley, if desired. Makes 4 to 6 servings.

Per serving: 248 calories, 35 g protein, 4 g carbohydrates, 9 g total fat, 125 mg cholesterol, 213 mg sodium

Sautéed Shrimp in Mint Beurre Blanc

Preparation time: About 15 minutes
Cooking time: About 10 minutes

Bright, cool mint adds snap to a rich butter sauce for shrimp. Spoon over a bed of rice and serve with sautéed cherry tomatoes.

- ■ ½ teaspoon grated lemon peel
- ■ 1 cup firmly packed fresh mint leaves
- ■ 6 tablespoons butter or margarine
- ■ 1 to 1½ pounds medium-size raw shrimp, shelled and deveined
- ■ 1 cup dry white wine
  Lemon slices and mint sprigs (optional)

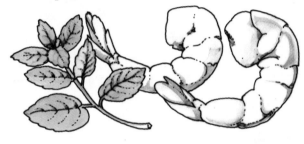

1 In a food processor or blender, whirl lemon peel, mint, and 4 tablespoons of the butter until blended. Set aside. Rinse shrimp and pat dry.

2 In a wide frying pan, melt remaining 2 tablespoons butter over medium heat. Add shrimp and cook, stirring, until shrimp turn bright pink and are opaque in thickest part when cut (about 5 minutes). Transfer to a warm serving platter; keep warm.

3 Add wine to pan and boil over high heat, stirring, until liquid is reduced to ⅓ cup (about 5 minutes). Add mint butter all at once and cook, stirring, just until sauce is smooth and slightly thickened. Remove from heat. Pour sauce over shrimp and garnish with lemon slices and mint sprigs, if desired. Makes 4 servings.

Per serving: 256 calories, 19 g protein, 2 g carbohydrates, 19 g total fat, 186 mg cholesterol, 315 mg sodium

Stir-fried Shrimp with Green Onions

Preparation time: About 10 minutes
Cooking time: About 4 minutes

For a Chinese-style feast, offer this exquisite stir-fry with steamed rice and ginger-seasoned cooked carrots. Prepare all the ingredients before starting, because stir-frying goes quickly.

- ■ 1 pound large raw shrimp, shelled and deveined
- ■ 1 tablespoon rice wine or dry sherry
- ■ 1 tablespoon cornstarch
- ■ 2 tablespoons salad oil
- ■ 4 green onions (including tops), thinly sliced
  Soy sauce (optional)

1 Rinse shrimp and pat dry. In a small bowl, mix shrimp with wine and cornstarch.

2 Set a wok or wide frying pan over high heat. When pan is hot, add oil, swirling to coat. When oil is hot, add shrimp mixture and cook, stirring, until shrimp turn bright pink (2 to 3 minutes).

3 Add onions and continue to cook, stirring, until shrimp are opaque in thickest part when cut (about 1 more minute). Transfer to a serving bowl. Offer soy sauce to add to taste, if desired. Makes 3 servings.

Per serving: 227 calories, 25 g protein, 5 g carbohydrates, 11 g total fat, 186 mg cholesterol, 183 mg sodium

Scallops with Shallot Butter

Preparation time: About 15 minutes
Baking time: 6 to 8 minutes

Cloaked in an aromatic butter sauce, sea scallops present an impressive entrée. Look for scallop shells in cookware shops—or use shallow baking or gratin dishes. Broiled tomatoes add color to each plate.

- **20 sea scallops (about 1 lb. *total*)**
- **⅓ cup butter or margarine, at room temperature**
- **⅓ cup minced shallots**
- **2 cloves garlic, minced or pressed**
- **2 tablespoons minced parsley**
  Freshly ground white pepper
  Lemon wedges (optional)

1 Rinse scallops and pat dry. Divide among 4 scallop shells or 5- to 6-inch shallow baking or gratin dishes.

2 In a small bowl, mix butter, shallots, garlic, and parsley until well blended. Evenly dot scallops with shallot butter and season to taste with white pepper.

3 Set shells in a baking pan just large enough to hold them. Bake on top rack of a 500° oven until scallops are opaque in center when cut (6 to 8 minutes). Garnish with lemon, if desired. Makes 4 servings.

Per serving: 246 calories, 20 g protein, 6 g carbohydrates, 16 g total fat, 78 mg cholesterol, 340 mg sodium

Oysters Calico

Preparation time: About 10 minutes
Cooking time: About 25 minutes

For a shellfish dish sure to attract attention, spoon broiled oysters onto toasted English muffins for breakfast, lunch, or dinner.

- **8 slices bacon**
- **1 medium-size green bell pepper, stemmed, seeded, and chopped**
- **1 medium-size onion, chopped**
- **2 pounds shucked oysters, drained**
- **1 cup (4 oz.) shredded Cheddar cheese**

1 In a wide frying pan, cook bacon over medium-high heat until crisp (about 7 minutes). Lift out, drain, and crumble; set aside. Discard all but 2 tablespoons of the drippings from pan.

2 Add bell pepper and onion to pan. Cook, stirring occasionally, until vegetables are soft (about 7 minutes). Set aside.

3 Rinse oysters in a colander and pat dry. Arrange snugly in a single layer in a shallow ovenproof serving dish. Broil about 4 inches below heat until edges of oysters begin to curl; turn over and broil until edges curl again (about 6 minutes total).

4 Evenly spoon onion mixture over oysters; sprinkle with bacon and cheese. Return to broiler and broil just until cheese is melted (1 to 2 minutes). Makes 4 to 6 servings.

Per serving: 237 calories, 18 g protein, 8 g carbohydrates, 14 g total fat, 110 mg cholesterol, 422 mg sodium

Mussels Marinière

Pictured facing page

Preparation time: About 15 minutes
Cooking time: About 7 minutes

Of the many tempting mussel recipes from France, this may be the most inspired. Steamed in a subtle wine broth, the shellfish develop eloquent flavor. Offer with crusty bread to catch the delicate juices.

- 3 **to 4 pounds mussels, scrubbed**
- 3 **tablespoons butter or margarine**
- 4 **green onions (including tops), thinly sliced**
- 1 **clove garlic, minced or pressed**
- 1 **cup dry white wine**
- ½ **cup lightly packed minced parsley**
- ⅛ **teaspoon pepper**

 Discard any mussels that do not close when tapped. Tear beard (clump of fibers along side of shell) off each mussel with a quick tug. Set mussels aside.

2. In a 4- to 6-quart pan, melt butter over medium heat. Add onions and garlic and cook, stirring occasionally, until soft (about 2 minutes). Add wine, parsley, and pepper; bring to a boil over high heat. Add mussels; reduce heat, cover, and simmer until mussels open (about 5 minutes). Discard any unopened shells.

3. With a slotted spoon, transfer mussels to individual serving bowls; evenly pour cooking liquid over each portion. Makes 4 servings.

Per serving: 171 calories, 12 g protein, 6 g carbohydrates, 11 g total fat, 51 mg cholesterol, 378 mg sodium

Steamed Soft-shell Crab with Ginger Sauce

Preparation time: About 15 minutes
Cooking time: About 8 minutes

Delectable and wholly edible, soft-shell crabs are available fresh during the summer and frozen the rest of the year. Have fresh crabs cleaned by your fishmonger (frozen ones have already been cleaned). They're small, so offer 2 or 3 per serving, with crisp potato chips and cold beer.

- 6 **cleaned soft-shell blue crabs (about 2 oz. *each*), thawed if frozen**
- ⅓ **cup rice wine vinegar**
- 1 **to 2 tablespoons sliced green onion (including top)**
- 1½ **tablespoons minced fresh ginger**
- 1 **teaspoon sugar**

1 Place a steamer rack over 1 to 2 inches boiling water in a large pan or wok. Lay crabs, back sides up, in a single layer on rack. Cover and steam over high heat until crabs are opaque in center of body when cut (about 8 minutes).

 Meanwhile, stir together vinegar, onion, ginger, and sugar in a small bowl.

3 Transfer crabs to warm plates. Offer ginger sauce to spoon over each portion. Makes 2 or 3 servings.

Per serving: 122 calories, 22 g protein, 3 g carbohydrates, 2 g total fat, 108 mg cholesterol, 305 mg sodium

A spectacular presentation that requires little
effort, Mussels Marinière (recipe on facing page)
steam in a wine-infused broth. Provide crusty
bread to dip in the delectable juices.

Quick Touches of Flavor

You don't have to be a magician to create these wonderful condiments in the wink of an eye. A spoonful here or a cupful there can transform plain pasta, meats, or fruit into mesmerizing treats.

Each recipe suggests its uses; let your taste buds tell you how much to apply. Expect to be spellbound by the effect.

Fresh Pineapple Salsa

- 1 small pineapple (about 3½ lbs.)
- 1 medium-size red onion, minced
- ¾ cup finely chopped fresh cilantro (coriander)
- 1 tablespoon white wine vinegar
- ½ teaspoon liquid hot pepper seasoning

1 Cut off top of pineapple. With a grapefruit knife, cut fruit from shell in chunks (reserving shell, if desired) and coarsely chop; drain off liquid. In a bowl, stir together fruit, onion, cilantro, vinegar, and hot pepper seasoning. Spoon into pineapple shell, if desired. Makes 3 cups.

Suggested uses: Spoon on roast pork or chops, ham steaks, or grilled fish; or serve with jicama sticks and bell pepper spears for dipping.

Per tablespoon: 9 calories, 0.1 g protein, 2 g carbohydrates, 0.1 g total fat, 0 mg cholesterol, 2 mg sodium

Parmesan-Herb Croutons

- ½ pound day-old French bread
- ¼ cup butter or margarine
- 1 tablespoon grated Parmesan cheese
- 1 teaspoon herbes de Provence or Italian herb seasoning

1 Cut bread into ½-inch cubes. Spread on a large rimmed baking sheet and bake in a 300° oven for 15 minutes.

2 In a wide frying pan, melt butter over medium-high heat. Add bread cubes, cheese, and herbs; mix gently until bread cubes are evenly coated and butter is absorbed (about 2 minutes). Remove from heat and let cool. Makes about 3 cups.

Suggested uses: Toss into salads, sprinkle over soups, or use as stuffing for poultry or fish.

Per ¼ cup: 91 calories, 2 g protein, 11 g carbohydrates, 5 g total fat, 11 mg cholesterol, 158 mg sodium

Pesto

- 2 **cups lightly packed fresh basil leaves**
- 1 **cup (5 oz.) grated Parmesan cheese**
- ½ to ⅔ **cup olive oil**
- 1 **or 2 cloves garlic**

1 In a blender or food processor, whirl basil, cheese, ½ cup of the oil, and garlic until puréed; if too thick, add more oil. Makes 1½ cups.

Suggested uses: Stir into hot pasta, spread on toasted bread and top with tomatoes, add to vegetable soups, or blend into scrambled eggs.

Per tablespoon: 71 calories, 3 g protein, 1 g carbohydrates, 6 g total fat, 5 mg cholesterol, 111 mg sodium

Cumin-Garlic Yogurt Sauce

- 1½ **cups plain yogurt**
- 2 **tablespoons minced fresh cilantro (coriander)**
- 1 **clove garlic, minced or pressed**
- 1 **teaspoon cumin seeds**

1 Stir together yogurt, cilantro, garlic, and cumin seeds. Cover and refrigerate for 15 minutes before using. Makes about 1½ cups.

Suggested uses: Spoon over cooked fish or chicken, boiled couscous, or sliced cucumbers or tomatoes.

Per tablespoon: 9 calories, 0.8 g protein, 1 g carbohydrates, 0.2 g total fat, 0.9 mg cholesterol, 10 mg sodium

Mignonette Sauce

- ¼ **cup** *each* **white wine vinegar and dry white wine**
- 1 **tablespoon minced red onion**
- ½ **teaspoon coarsely ground black pepper**

1 Stir together vinegar, wine, onion, and pepper. Transfer to small bowls for dipping, if desired. Makes about ½ cup.

Suggested uses: Spoon over raw oysters or use as a dip for cooked shellfish or grilled sausages.

Per tablespoon: 7 calories, 0 g protein, 0.5 g carbohydrates, 0 g total fat, 0 mg cholesterol, 0.4 mg sodium

Spiced Apple Honey

- 1 **cup whipped honey**
- 2 **tablespoons spiced apple butter**
- ½ **teaspoon ground nutmeg**
- ¼ **teaspoon ground cinnamon**

1 Stir together honey, apple butter, nutmeg, and cinnamon until blended. Makes 1 cup.

Suggested uses: Spread on warm toast, stir into hot cereal, or smear on baked fruit.

Per tablespoon: 37 calories, 0 g protein, 10 g carbohydrates, 0 g total fat, 0 mg cholesterol, 0.6 mg sodium

Caramel Sauce

- ½ **cup sugar**
- ¼ **cup water**
- **Pinch of cream of tartar**
- ½ **cup whipping cream**

1 In a deep, heavy 2- to 3-quart pan, gently stir together sugar, water, and cream of tartar. Set over low heat and cook, stirring, until sugar is dissolved. Increase heat to high and boil until syrup is a deep golden color (about 10 minutes).

2 Remove from heat and immediately pour in cream (mixture will bubble vigorously); stir with a wooden spoon until blended. Let cool for at least 10 minutes before using. Makes about 1 cup.

Suggested uses: Pour over ice cream, baked apples or pears, or pound cake; or use as a dip for dried fruits and nuts.

Per tablespoon: 46 calories, 0.2 g protein, 6 g carbohydrates, 2 g total fat, 8 mg cholesterol, 3 mg sodium

Glorious green spears banded with a citrus beurre
blanc, Asparagus with Orange-Butter Sauce (recipe
on facing page) presents a side dish that's sure
to attract attention.

Side Dishes

Mealtime excitement may focus on the main dish, but it doesn't have to stop there. Add interest to any plate with an elegant vegetable, potato, or grain accompaniment.

On these pages we offer colorful and enticing side-dish possibilities. Some are sturdy enough to serve solo; others turn a plain menu into a sophisticated event. All are so effortless to make that they can be included even on busy nights.

Asparagus with Orange-Butter Sauce
Pictured on facing page

Preparation time: About 10 minutes
Cooking time: About 12 minutes

Crisp asparagus spears cloaked with a rich butter sauce are a stunning complement to Pounded Lamb Chops with Rosemary (page 53), Game Hens with Mustard Crust (page 55), or any other elegant entrée.

- 2 pounds asparagus, tough ends removed
- 8 tablespoons butter or margarine
- ⅓ cup minced shallots
- 1¼ teaspoons Dijon mustard
- 1⅓ cups freshly squeezed orange juice
  Strips of orange peel tied in knots or orange slices (optional)

1. In a wide frying pan, bring 1 inch water to a boil over high heat. Add asparagus; reduce heat and simmer, uncovered, until barely tender when pierced (3 to 5 minutes); drain. Place asparagus on a warm serving platter and keep warm.

2. In a 1- to 2-quart pan, melt 1 tablespoon of the butter over medium heat. Add shallots and cook, stirring, for 1 minute. Add mustard and orange juice, increase heat to high, and boil, uncovered, until reduced to ⅔ cup (about 5 minutes). Reduce heat to low, add remaining 7 tablespoons butter all at once, and cook, stirring constantly, until butter is melted and sauce is smooth. Spoon sauce over asparagus and garnish with orange peel, if desired. Makes 6 servings.

Per serving: 186 calories, 3 g protein, 10 g carbohydrates, 16 g total fat, 41 mg cholesterol, 191 mg sodium

Risotto-style Corn

Preparation time: About 10 minutes
Cooking time: 15 to 20 minutes

Fresh corn kernels become delectably creamy when cooked risotto style (similar to the Italian rice classic described on page 37). The result makes a superb partner to grilled meats or a simple vegetarian meal when combined with a tomato salad and toasted bread slices.

- 6 ears of corn
- 2 tablespoons butter or margarine
- 1 large red onion, chopped
- 1 red bell pepper, stemmed, seeded, and chopped
- 2 cups whipping cream
- 1 teaspoon sugar
  Salt and pepper

1. Pull off and discard husks and silk from corn; rinse cobs. With a sharp knife, cut off kernels; set aside.

2. In a wide frying pan, melt butter over medium-high heat. Add onion and bell pepper and cook, stirring often, until soft (about 5 minutes). Add corn, cream, and sugar. Cook, stirring constantly, until mixture is thickened (10 to 15 minutes). Season to taste with salt and pepper. Transfer to a warm serving bowl. Makes 6 servings.

Per serving: 359 calories, 5 g protein, 23 g carbohydrates, 30 g total fat, 99 mg cholesterol, 81 mg sodium

Sautéed Peppers & Pears

Pictured on page 51

Preparation time: About 10 minutes
Cooking time: About 10 minutes

This fresh and vivid mélange marries the natural sweetness of pears and red bell peppers. It adds a festive accent to any menu that features ham, pork, or turkey. As a variation, substitute sliced apples for the pears.

- 3 tablespoons butter or margarine
- 4 medium-size red or yellow bell peppers or a combination of both (about 1 lb. *total*), stemmed, seeded, and cut into ¼-inch strips
- 3 medium-size firm-ripe pears or Golden Delicious apples, peeled, cored, and sliced ¼ inch thick
- ¾ cup (3 oz.) shredded jack or Münster cheese (optional)

1. In a wide frying pan, melt 1½ tablespoons of the butter over medium heat. Add bell peppers and cook, stirring often, until limp (about 5 minutes).

2. Add pears and remaining 1½ tablespoons butter. Cook, stirring often, until fruit is tender (about 5 more minutes).

3. Pour into a warm serving dish. Immediately sprinkle with cheese, if desired. Makes 6 servings.

Per serving: 115 calories, 1 g protein, 16 g carbohydrates, 6 g total fat, 16 mg cholesterol, 60 mg sodium

Minted
Lettuce & Peas

Preparation time: About 7 minutes
Cooking time: About 2 minutes

Create a small sensation by serving lettuce cups that cradle lemon- and mint-seasoned peas with Chutney Chicken (page 57) or broiled lamb chops.

- **1 small head (about 5 oz.) red leaf lettuce, washed and dried**
- **2 tablespoons butter or margarine**
- **1 package (10 oz.) frozen tiny peas, thawed**
- **¼ cup chopped fresh mint leaves or 1½ tablespoons dry mint leaves**
- **2 teaspoons grated lemon peel**
  Salt and pepper

1 Set aside 6 large lettuce leaves; cut remaining lettuce into thin strips.

2 In a wide frying pan, melt butter over medium-high heat. Add peas and lettuce strips; cook, stirring, until lettuce is wilted (about 2 minutes). Stir in mint and lemon peel. Season to taste with salt and pepper.

3 Place a whole lettuce leaf on each of 6 plates. Spoon pea mixture equally into center of each leaf. Makes 6 servings.

Per serving: 70 calories, 3 g protein, 6 g carbohydrates, 4 g total fat, 10 mg cholesterol, 105 mg sodium

Eggplant with
Crispy Coating

Preparation time: About 10 minutes
Baking time: 20 to 25 minutes

Crunchy on the outside, soft in the center, and full of herbal flavor, these coated eggplant slices wonderfully enhance pork chops or Turkey Scaloppine (page 58). Or top with your favorite tomato sauce and serve as a main dish.

- **1 large eggplant (1 to 1½ lbs.)**
- **2 eggs**
- **½ cup fine dry bread crumbs or yellow cornmeal**
- **1 teaspoon dry oregano leaves**
- **¼ cup grated Parmesan cheese**
- **2 tablespoons olive oil or salad oil**

1 Cut stem off eggplant; peel, if desired. Cut crosswise into ½-inch-thick slices. Set aside.

2 Lightly beat eggs in a shallow bowl. In another shallow bowl, mix bread crumbs, oregano, and cheese.

3 Spread oil in a rimmed baking pan large enough to hold eggplant in a single layer. Dip each eggplant slice in eggs, drain briefly, and then coat with crumb mixture, shaking off excess. Arrange in pan.

4 Bake in a 425° oven, turning once, until browned and very soft when pressed (20 to 25 minutes total). Transfer to a warm serving platter. Makes 4 to 6 servings.

Per serving: 131 calories, 5 g protein, 10 g carbohydrates, 8 g total fat, 94 mg cholesterol, 149 mg sodium

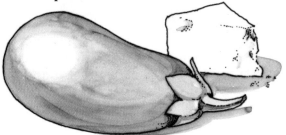

Trio of Sautéed Mushrooms

Preparation time: About 15 minutes
Cooking time: About 20 minutes

With the enticing variety of mushrooms available today, it's time to honor them in a dish of their own. Their earthy, oaky flavor provides a perfect foil for Pork Tenderloins with Stilton & Port (page 50) or any roast pork or fowl.

- 1 ounce *each* dried cèpes (also called porcini) and dried chanterelle mushrooms (or 2 oz. *total* of either)
- 5 tablespoons butter or margarine
- 1½ pounds fresh regular mushrooms, cleaned and sliced
- ¼ teaspoon dry thyme leaves

1 Soak dried mushrooms in very hot tap water to cover for 10 minutes. Drain in a colander and rinse well with cool water; drain again. Set aside.

2 In a wide frying pan, melt 3 tablespoons of the butter over medium-high heat. Add regular mushrooms and cook, stirring often, until mushrooms are soft and liquid has evaporated (about 15 minutes).

3 Melt remaining 2 tablespoons butter in pan. Add cèpes, chanterelles, and thyme. Cook, stirring, until mushrooms are lightly browned (about 5 minutes). Transfer to a warm serving bowl. Makes about 6 servings.

Per serving: 140 calories, 3 g protein, 12 g carbohydrates, 10 g total fat, 26 mg cholesterol, 106 mg sodium

Bacon Polenta

Pictured on facing page

Preparation time: About 10 minutes
Cooking time: About 15 minutes

Hearty polenta, dressed up with bacon, onion, and garlic, adds gusto to meat and poultry dinners. Or serve with nothing more than a green salad. Look for polenta—coarsely ground Italian-style cornmeal—in Italian delicatessens and some supermarkets.

- 5 slices bacon, chopped
- ⅓ cup finely chopped onion
- 2 large cloves garlic, minced or pressed
- 2¼ cups regular-strength chicken broth
- ¾ cup polenta or yellow cornmeal
  Salt

1 In a 2- to 3-quart pan, cook bacon over medium heat, stirring, until lightly browned (about 5 minutes). Add onion and garlic and cook, stirring, until onion is limp and bacon is well browned (about 5 more minutes). Discard all but 1 tablespoon of the drippings from pan.

2 Add 1½ cups of the broth to pan and bring to a boil over high heat. Meanwhile, mix polenta with remaining ¾ cup broth in a small bowl.

3 Using a long-handled spoon, stir polenta mixture into boiling broth (mixture will thicken and spatter). Reduce heat to low and cook, stirring constantly, for 5 minutes. Season to taste with salt. Spoon into a warm serving dish. Makes 4 servings.

Per serving: 189 calories, 6 g protein, 23 g carbohydrates, 8 g total fat, 9 mg cholesterol, 708 mg sodium

Piping hot from the pan, golden Bacon Polenta
(recipe on facing page) satisfies hungry appetites,
whether it's served solo or as an accompaniment to
roasted meats and poultry.

Hashed-brown Zucchini

Preparation time: About 20 minutes
Cooking time: About 12 minutes

Sometimes, great recipes are born from reinventing an old favorite. That's what happened when we substituted shredded zucchini in this popular potato dish. Serve with sausages for breakfast or with roast meat for dinner.

- 1½ **pounds zucchini, ends trimmed**
- ½ **teaspoon salt**
- 2 **eggs**
- 6 **tablespoons grated Parmesan cheese**
- 1 **clove garlic, minced or pressed**
- **About 4 tablespoons butter or margarine**
- **Tomato wedges (optional)**

1 Coarsely shred zucchini (you should have about 4 cups) and combine with salt in a medium-size bowl. Let stand for about 15 minutes. Squeeze with your hands to press out moisture. Stir in eggs, cheese, and garlic.

2 In a wide frying pan, melt 2 tablespoons of the butter over medium-high heat. Spoon about 2 tablespoons of the zucchini mixture into pan in a mound; flatten slightly. Continue making patties, without crowding, and cook, turning once, until golden (about 6 minutes total). Lift out and arrange on a warm serving platter; keep warm. Repeat to cook remaining zucchini mixture, adding more butter as needed. Garnish with tomatoes, if desired. Makes 4 servings.

Per serving: 175 calories, 8 g protein, 6 g carbohydrates, 14 g total fat, 166 mg cholesterol, 541 mg sodium

Sautéed Kale
with Cannellini Beans

Preparation time: About 10 minutes
Cooking time: About 20 minutes

Often overlooked, kale offers bold flavor, substantial nutritive value, and satisfying texture when cooked. Added to cannellini beans and bacon in this robust preparation, it lends a tasty accent to barbecued ribs or chicken.

- 1½ **pounds kale, tough stems trimmed**
- 4 **slices bacon, chopped**
- 2 **large onions, thinly sliced**
- **Salt and pepper**
- 2 **cans (1 lb. *each*) cannellini (white kidney) beans, drained**

1 Rinse and drain kale. Cut crosswise into ½-inch strips and set aside.

2 In a wide frying pan, cook bacon over medium-high heat, stirring, until crisp (about 7 minutes). Lift out, drain, and set aside.

3 Add onions to pan and cook, stirring, until soft (about 5 minutes). Add kale and cook, stirring, until wilted and bright green (3 to 4 minutes). Season to taste with salt and pepper. Transfer to a warm serving platter and keep warm.

4 Add beans to pan, reduce heat, and cook, stirring, until hot (about 4 minutes). Arrange beans alongside kale; sprinkle both with bacon. Makes 6 servings.

Per serving: 200 calories, 12 g protein, 33 g carbohydrates, 3 g total fat, 4 mg cholesterol, 624 mg sodium

Spiced Spinach & Potatoes

Preparation time: About 10 minutes
Cooking time: 25 to 30 minutes

Subtly spiced and fragrant, this earthy dish of diced potatoes and spinach is also quite substantial. Just add cooked meat or chicken for a complete entrée.

- 4 tablespoons salad oil
- 2 large russet potatoes (about 1¼ lbs. *total*), peeled and cut into ½-inch cubes
- ¾ pound spinach, stems removed
- 2 cloves garlic, minced or pressed
- 2 teaspoons ground coriander
- ½ teaspoon ground ginger

1 Heat 3 tablespoons of the oil in a wide frying pan over medium-high heat. When oil is hot, add potatoes and cook, stirring occasionally, until browned on most sides (10 to 15 minutes). Meanwhile, cut spinach leaves crosswise into ½-inch strips. Wash and drain well; set aside.

2 Reduce heat to low; add garlic, coriander, ginger, and remaining 1 tablespoon oil to potatoes and cook, stirring, until very fragrant (2 to 3 minutes). Pour in ½ cup water, cover, and simmer until potatoes are tender when pierced (about 8 minutes); add more water, if necessary, to prevent sticking.

3 Add spinach to pan, increase heat to high, and cook, stirring, until leaves are wilted and most of the liquid has evaporated (about 2 minutes). Transfer to a warm serving platter. Makes 4 servings.

Per serving: 241 calories, 4 g protein, 26 g carbohydrates, 14 g total fat, 0 mg cholesterol, 59 mg sodium

Best-ever Garlicky Potatoes

Preparation time: About 10 minutes
Baking time: About 23 minutes

We don't mean to brag, but we're sure you'll agree that these potatoes are irresistible, especially alongside meat or poultry. Choose an entrée, such as Baked Pork Chops Dijon (page 50), that you can roast in the same oven.

- 1 tablespoon olive oil
- 1 tablespoon butter or margarine
- 3 large red thin-skinned potatoes (about 1 lb. *total*), cut into eighths
- 1 medium-size onion, cut into eighths
- 3 cloves garlic, halved
  Salt and pepper

1 Place oil and butter in a medium-size baking pan and heat in a 475° oven until butter is melted and sizzling (about 3 minutes).

2 Add potatoes, onion, and garlic to pan and stir well. Continue to bake, stirring occasionally, until potatoes are golden brown and tender (about 20 minutes). Season to taste with salt and pepper. Makes 2 to 4 servings.

Per serving: 157 calories, 3 g protein, 23 g carbohydrates, 7 g total fat, 8 mg cholesterol, 39 mg sodium

A sweet indulgence that you can assemble at the
last minute, rich and silken Spirited Chocolate
Fondue (recipe on facing page) brings any dinner
party to a delightful conclusion.

Desserts

Virtually everyone loves dessert. Whether you crave a slice of lavish chocolate cake or a tree-ripened peach is a matter of individual taste. But it's the sweet indulgence that makes you feel good. Recipes in this chapter celebrate this delight with fresh berries, comforting cooked fruit, rich chocolate, and sweet sugar and cream creations. Share some of the goodness and present delectable desserts that are deceptively easy to prepare for company events or everyday meals.

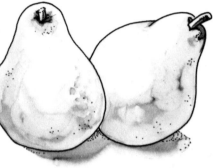

Spirited Chocolate Fondue

Pictured on facing page

Preparation time: About 15 minutes
Cooking time: About 10 minutes

Discover the luxury of dipping fresh fruit into chocolate fondue (you can also dip ladyfingers or cubes of pound cake). A splash of orange liqueur gives this version a spirited kick.

- **1 pound bittersweet, semisweet, or milk chocolate (or a mixture of all three), coarsely chopped**
- **1 cup whipping cream**
- **¼ cup orange-flavored liqueur**
- **1 pound mixed fresh fruit, such as washed and hulled strawberries, peeled and cubed melon, banana slices, and pear slices**
  Lemon juice (optional)

1 Combine chocolate and cream in a medium-size metal bowl or in top of a double boiler. Place container over a pan of simmering water and stir just until chocolate is melted (about 10 minutes). Stir in liqueur. Transfer chocolate mixture to a chafing dish or fondue pot and set over low heat.

2 If using bananas or pears, brush cut sides of fruit with lemon juice to prevent darkening. Arrange fruit in separate groups on a serving platter alongside fondue. Offer skewers for dipping fruit into chocolate. Makes 8 to 10 servings.

Per serving: 318 calories, 4 g protein, 30 g carbohydrates, 26 g total fat, 27 mg cholesterol, 11 mg sodium

Pecan Graham Crisps

Preparation time: About 20 minutes
Cooking time: About 10 minutes

Chewy toffee and rich chocolate top graham crackers in this easy-to-make confection. Serve with milk, coffee, or tea whenever you crave an effortless sweet nibble. You'll need a candy thermometer to make the toffee.

- 12 **whole graham crackers (2½ by 4¾ inches)**
- 1 **cup (½ lb.) butter or margarine**
- 1¼ **cups firmly packed light brown sugar**
- 1 **cup finely chopped pecans or walnuts**
- 1 **teaspoon vanilla**
- 1 **cup (6 oz.) semisweet or milk chocolate chips**

1 Place crackers side by side in a single layer in a 10- by 15-inch baking pan. Set aside.

2 In a 1- to 2-quart pan, melt butter over medium heat. Stir in sugar and nuts; cook, stirring often, until mixture comes to a boil. Continue to boil until mixture reaches 238°F on a candy thermometer (4 to 5 minutes). Remove from heat, stir in vanilla, and immediately pour over crackers, spreading to cover completely.

3 Bake in a 375° oven until very bubbly (about 5 minutes). Remove and immediately sprinkle with chocolate; let stand until melted (2 to 3 minutes). Spread over topping. Cut into 24 squares; then cut each square in half diagonally. Let cool for at least 10 minutes. Makes 4 dozen crisps.

Per crisp: 95 calories, 0.5 g protein, 9 g carbohydrates, 7 g total fat, 10 mg cholesterol, 53 mg sodium

Warm Fruit Gratin with Zabaglione

Preparation time: About 10 minutes
Cooking time: 4 to 6 minutes

It may be hard to spell or to say, but zabaglione ("sah-be-YO-nay") isn't complicated to make. A warm froth of eggs, wine, and sugar, it cloaks summer fruits and then is broiled until golden.

- **About 5 cups fruit, such as hulled strawberries, blueberries, or sliced peaches, or a combination**
- 3 **eggs**
- 6 **tablespoons granulated sugar**
- 2 **tablespoons fruity white wine, such as Johannisberg Riesling**
- 2 **tablespoons *each* powdered sugar and sliced almonds**

1 Rinse and drain fruit. Divide among 4 to 6 shallow, ovenproof wide-rimmed bowls. Position broiler rack so tops of bowls will be about 4 inches below heat. Set bowls aside.

2 In a round-bottomed zabaglione pan or top of a double boiler, beat eggs, granulated sugar, and wine until frothy. Place container over a pan of simmering water and beat rapidly until tripled in volume (3 to 5 minutes).

3 Immediately pour zabaglione over fruit. Dust with powdered sugar and sprinkle with almonds. Broil until golden brown (about 1 minute). Makes 4 to 6 servings.

Per serving: 147 calories, 4 g protein, 25 g carbohydrates, 4 g total fat, 137 mg cholesterol, 36 mg sodium

Peach Brûlée

Preparation time: About 15 minutes
Cooking time: About 3 minutes

Crème brûlée, a classic French custard, has a delicious crackly topping of caramelized sugar. Borrow the idea and crown blueberry-filled peaches with a similar cooked sugar crust.

- Butter or margarine
- 2 tablespoons lemon juice
- 3 large ripe peaches, peeled, halved, and pitted
- ½ cup blueberries
- 6 tablespoons firmly packed brown sugar
- ⅓ to ½ cup sour cream

1 Melt 2 tablespoons of the butter and mix with lemon juice; coat peach halves with butter mixture and place, cut sides up, on a large baking sheet. Fill each cavity with 1 tablespoon of the blueberries; set remaining berries aside.

2 Line another large baking sheet with foil and butter generously. Push about 1 tablespoon of the brown sugar through a wire sieve onto foil, making an even layer about 3 inches square; repeat to make 6 squares total.

3 Broil sugar about 6 inches below heat just until melted (1 to 2 minutes). Let cool until set but still pliable (about 30 seconds).

4 With a wide spatula, set a sugar square on each peach half. Broil about 6 inches below heat just until sugar crust drapes around peach (10 to 30 seconds). Transfer peach halves to dessert plates. Garnish each portion with sour cream and remaining berries. Makes 6 servings.

Per serving: 155 calories, 1 g protein, 25 g carbohydrates, 7 g total fat, 16 mg cholesterol, 52 mg sodium

Baked Pears with Anise Seeds

Preparation time: About 7 minutes
Baking time: About 25 minutes

As a foil to delicate pears, anise seeds add a spicy dimension to this baked dessert. Accompany with a late-harvest Riesling for a special occasion.

- 4 medium-size firm-ripe Comice or d'Anjou pears, peeled
- ¼ cup *each* hot water and firmly packed brown sugar
- 2 tablespoons butter or margarine, melted
- ¼ teaspoon anise seeds

1 Set pears upright in a shallow baking pan just large enough to hold them.

2 In a small bowl, mix water, sugar, butter, and anise seeds. Pour over pears. Bake in a 375° oven, basting occasionally with pan juices, until pears are tender (about 25 minutes). Transfer pears to dessert bowls and drizzle with pan juices. Makes 4 servings.

Per serving: 200 calories, 0.7 g protein, 38 g carbohydrates, 6 g total fat, 16 mg cholesterol, 63 mg sodium

Cider-poached Apples with Yogurt

Preparation time: About 7 minutes
Cooking time: 24 to 27 minutes

Instead of baking, try poaching apples in cider. It creates a fragrant sauce to spoon over each serving of fruit. Cool yogurt and crunchy pecans add appetizing contrast.

- 1 quart apple cider or juice
- 4 medium-size McIntosh or Golden Delicious apples
- ½ to ¾ cup plain or vanilla-flavored yogurt
- ½ cup chopped pecans

1 In a 2- to 3-quart pan, boil apple cider, uncovered, over high heat until reduced to 1 cup (about 12 minutes). Meanwhile, core apples.

2 Add apples to cider and return to a boil. Reduce heat, cover, and simmer until apples are tender (12 to 15 minutes). Transfer apples to dessert bowls and spoon sauce over each portion. Top each apple with yogurt and nuts. Makes 4 servings.

Per serving: 306 calories, 3 g protein, 54 g carbohydrates, 10 g total fat, 2 mg cholesterol, 27 mg sodium

Salzburger Nockerln

Pictured on facing page

Preparation time: About 15 minutes
Baking time: 10 to 12 minutes

From Austria comes this light and billowy dessert. Deceptively easy to prepare, it makes a dramatic offering when presented warm and golden from the oven.

- 1 ounce semisweet chocolate
- 4 eggs, separated
- ¼ cup sugar
- 4 teaspoons all-purpose flour
- 1 tablespoon butter or margarine

1 Using a vegetable peeler, shave chocolate firmly. Set shavings aside.

2 In large bowl of an electric mixer, beat egg whites until soft peaks form. Gradually add sugar, beating until very stiff. Set aside.

3 With same beater, beat egg yolks at high speed in a small bowl until very light in color and slightly thickened. Gradually add flour, beating until mixture is thick and well blended. Fold yolks into whites, blending lightly but thoroughly.

4 In a shallow 2-quart oval or rectangular heatproof pan, melt butter directly over medium heat. Making 6 equal mounds, heap egg mixture into warm pan. Bake in a 350° oven until top is pale brown (10 to 12 minutes). Sprinkle with chocolate shavings. Makes 6 servings.

Per serving: 132 calories, 4 g protein, 13 g carbohydrates, 7 g total fat, 188 mg cholesterol, 66 mg sodium

Although this soufflélike cloud of eggs and sugar
looks difficult to make, it's actually quite easy.
And Salzburger Nockerln (recipe on facing page) is
easy on the waistline as well.

91

Vanilla Cloud with Berries

Preparation time: 15 minutes

An airy, sweet cheese whip sets off beautifully ripe berries. For a striking presentation, mound the berries and cheese mixture side by side in a bowl and garnish with mint.

- 1 **large package (8 oz.) cream cheese**
- ½ **cup sugar**
- 1 **vanilla bean (4 to 6 inches long) or 1 teaspoon vanilla extract**
- 2 **cups sour cream or plain yogurt**
- 8 **cups fresh berries, such as hulled strawberries, raspberries, or blackberries, washed and drained**
  Mint sprigs (optional)

1 In large bowl of an electric mixer, blend cream cheese and sugar. Slit vanilla bean lengthwise and scrape seeds into bowl with tip of a knife (or add vanilla extract). Beat until smooth and fluffy. With mixer on high, gradually add sour cream, mixing after each addition until smooth.

2 Mound berries onto one side of a wide bowl. Pour cheese mixture beside fruit. Garnish with mint sprigs, if desired. Spoon portions of fruit and cream into dessert bowls. Makes 8 to 10 servings.

Per serving: 254 calories, 4 g protein, 21 g carbohydrates, 18 g total fat, 45 mg cholesterol, 93 mg sodium

Grapefruit & Cherry Compote

Preparation time: About 20 minutes
Cooking time: About 10 minutes

Light and lively, this fresh fruit dessert brings a spicy meal to a refreshing conclusion. Enjoy it in summer when cherries are in season—and again in winter when imported cherries become available.

- 5 **medium-size pink grapefruit (about 4¼ lbs. *total*)**
- 1 **pound sweet dark cherries, pitted**
- ⅓ **cup orange-flavored liqueur**
- 2 **tablespoons sugar**
- 1½ **tablespoons honey**

1 Pare golden peel from 1 of the grapefruit, scraping away any white pith. Cut peel into long, thin slivers. Place in a 1½- to 2-quart pan with 1 cup water. Bring to a boil over high heat; drain. Repeat. Set drained peel aside in pan.

2 Cut and discard peel and pith from remaining 4 grapefruit. Holding fruit over a bowl, cut between membrane to release segments into bowl. Squeeze juice from membrane into bowl; discard membrane. Drain off juice and reserve. Add cherries, ¼ cup of the liqueur, and 1 tablespoon of the sugar to grapefruit. Mix gently.

3 Add reserved juice, remaining 1 tablespoon sugar, and honey to peel in pan. Bring to a boil over high heat and cook, stirring often, until syrup is reduced to about 2 tablespoons (about 5 minutes). Stir in remaining liqueur.

4 Ladle fruit mixture into dessert bowls or goblets; top with peel and syrup. Makes 6 to 8 servings.

Per serving: 125 calories, 1 g protein, 27 g carbohydrates, 0.6 g total fat, 0 mg cholesterol, 0.2 mg sodium

Gingered Papaya Sundaes

Preparation time: About 10 minutes
Cooking time: 2 to 4 minutes

The subtle tropical sweetness of heated papaya, contrasted with cold vanilla ice cream, makes a wonderful finale to an Oriental meal.

- 1 firm-ripe papaya
- 2 or 3 large limes
- 2 tablespoons butter or margarine
- 2 tablespoons candied ginger, cut into thin strips
- 1 tablespoon firmly packed brown sugar
- Vanilla ice cream

1 Peel papaya and cut in half lengthwise; scoop out seeds. Cut papaya crosswise into ½-inch-thick slices.

2 Pare some thin outer green peel from 1 lime and cut into enough thin strips to make ½ teaspoon (or remove peel with a zesting tool). Ream enough fruit to make 2 tablespoons juice. Thinly slice remaining lime; set aside.

3 In a wide frying pan, melt butter over medium heat. Add papaya, ginger, and sugar. Cook, gently turning papaya, until hot (2 to 4 minutes). Stir in lime peel and lime juice. Spoon papaya onto dessert plates and moisten with pan juices. Top each portion with ice cream and lime slices. Makes 4 servings.

Per serving of sauce: 123 calories, 0.6 g protein, 18 g carbohydrates, 6 g total fat, 16 mg cholesterol, 67 mg sodium

Pear Fans
with Orange Syrup
Pictured on page 94

Preparation time: About 20 minutes

To show off rosy red Bartlett pears, fan out slender slices and place atop a warm orange syrup. Unlike the pears in many dessert recipes, the fruit is uncooked, yet the effect is elegant. (If red pears are not available, use any other variety.)

- ½ cup *each* sugar and orange juice
- ¼ cup butter or margarine
- 2 tablespoons lemon juice
- 1 teaspoon finely shredded orange or lemon peel
- 3 medium-size red Bartlett or other pears
  Additional shredded orange or lemon peel (optional)

1 In a 1- to 2-quart pan, combine sugar, orange juice, butter, and 1 tablespoon of the lemon juice; cook over high heat, stirring, until butter is melted. Stir in the 1 teaspoon peel and spoon sauce equally onto 6 dessert plates.

2 Cut pears in half lengthwise. Remove core and blossom end from each half. Cut each pear half lengthwise into ¼-inch slices, leaving stem end intact. Drizzle with remaining lemon juice.

3 Place a pear half, cut side down, on each plate. With flat of a knife, gently press down on each pear to fan out slices. Garnish with additional peel, if desired. Makes 6 servings.

Per serving: 192 calories, 0.6 g protein, 32 g carbohydrates, 8 g total fat, 21 mg cholesterol, 79 mg sodium

A showcase for the taste and glamour of red Bartletts,
Pear Fans with Orange Syrup (recipe on page 93) is
sophisticated in its simplicity, appealing in its
freshness. Try it with other pears, too.

INDEX